One Family's Triumph
Over Insurmountable Odds

YES WE CAN!

WALLY FROST

Regal
Books

A Division of G/L Publications
Ventura, CA U.S.A.

The foreign language publishing of all Regal books is under the direction of GLINT. GLINT provides financial and technical help for the adaptation, translation and publishing of books in more than 85 languages for millions of people worldwide.

For more information write: GLINT, P.O. Box 6688, Ventura, California 93006.

Published by Regal Books
A Division of GL Publications
Ventura, California 93006
Printed in U.S.A.

Library of Congress Cataloging in Publication Data

Frost, Wally, 1925-
  Yes We Can!

    1. Poliomyelitis—Patients—United States—Biography.   2. Frost, Wally, 1925-
I. Title.
RC180.2.F76   280'.4 [B]   81-51743
ISBN 0-8307-0799-9   AACR2

Contents

This book is gratefully dedicated to:
The memory of loving parents,
Ernest and Alta Frost,
and Nick Hibma;
To "Grandma" Hibma,
now in her nineties;
To my faithful, loyal, loving wife
Phyl;
To Dave, Dan, Steve, Becky and Debbie
and
To the glory of God!

Preface

"Yes, we can! Yes, we can! Yes, we can!" 41,498 screaming fans voiced their optimism.

The California Angels were on the verge of winning the West for the first time ever. The Angels had mathematically eliminated the Texas Rangers from the American League West race and now there were three—California, Kansas City and Minnesota. A festive air hung over the Big "A."

Angels players rushed toward the mound to congratulate the winning pitcher. Sprinting from the dugout, the manager got to him first. A boyish grin creased handsome Dave Frost's sweaty face. There was no doubt about it, he was a bonafide major leaguer now. After all, that win tied him with the fabled Nolan Ryan as the winningest Angels pitcher for the '79 season. He could be forgiven for feeling just a tinge of pride.

The organist had just finished a few bars of "Frosty, the Snowman." The fans were still hooting and cheering. It was a colorful montage of sights and sounds.

Probably the most deliriously happy fellow in the entire stadium was his dad. He was seated in a special section for wheelchairs graciously provided by the Angels' management, directly behind home plate. The wheelchair spectators frequently called out encouraging words and friendly jibes for the dad's benefit. A strikeout brought cheers while a ball elicited a "send him back to the minors." I think David Frost's dad should be forgiven for being a little indignant at the crowd's friendly catcalls and a wee bit proud of the cheers; especially since I'm his dad.

It's a long way from a dad's dream to the "Bigs." I suspect every father who enrolls his boy in a Little League program has an idea—oh, it may be ever so faint—but somewhere along the line, he entertains the notion that maybe, just maybe, it might be his kid that breaks it.

But the likelihood of that happening in our household seemed pretty remote. After all, most dads take the little guy to the local park and participate, demonstrate and encourage in a myriad of ways. Working through those seemingly insurmountable obstacles from a wheelchair has been an exciting adventure.

Long before the Angels' fans popularized that hypnotic chant at the Big "A," we quietly set about proving to ourselves, *Yes, we can!*

Acknowledgements

What? Me write a book? You must be joking!

I suppose I must have mentally picked up my pen innumerable times with the good intention of telling "my story." I dropped the idea equally as often. I was convinced that all of the books worth writing had already been written. There must be oodles of people "out there" with stories infinitely more interesting, exciting and graphic than anything I would have to tell—I thought.

But the requests kept coming. From the tranquil beaches of sunny California to the sandy wave-swept shores of Durban, South Africa, folks kept asking, "Why don't you write a book so we can read the whole story?"

Not until I received a call from Rod Toews, a friend of many years, did I seriously contemplate the idea. Even then I dragged my feet (figuratively speaking) for months. I want to thank Rod for his perseverance in encouraging me to make a try at it. I'm also grateful to Don Pugh and David Malme for their confidence and support throughout the project.

I want Carol Lacy, Regal's book editor, to know how much I appreciate her help in smoothing out the rough edges of the original manuscript. The hours spent discussing my "assumptions" were delightful.

Without the help of my charming, beautiful, and talented co-worker, my dear wife Phyllis, I doubt the task would ever have been finished. Her reading, rereading, checking my atrocious spelling and typing the "rough" proved to be an invaluable asset.

Since most events at our house are family affairs, this undertaking was no different. The whole family read all or portions of the draft before it was submitted. Their gentle, patient indulgence has been more than appreciated.

Most of all, I want to thank God for the exciting adventure through which He has led us all. Without Him, there would be no story. This is a story of the treasure of "miracle" children, of life reclaimed from the very pit of despair but more largely, an exciting odyssey of man's ultimate reason for passing through this veil of tears and distress—to know God.

Chapter 1
A Matter of Survival

Panic gripped my heart! My mind searched wildly for hope. The falling sensation turned to suspended animation as I waited to plunge beneath the icy surface.

Oh, God! I thought. *Why haven't I been a better boy? Why is my life going to end before I've even had a chance to shoot a gun or fly an airplane or . . . ?*

Our primitive, isolated farm in southern Minnesota was not without stark adventures for a 10-year-old boy. Alexander Graham Bell's wonderful invention had not yet reached beyond the tiny hamlets of the area and Thomas Edison would have been appalled to know that electricity for his mysterious, glowing globe was still more than two miles from our humble farm cottage.

And running water? The Saturday night bath was a dreaded ordeal, especially in the dead of winter. Dad carried a stone-cold galvanized washtub into the house and set it down near the wood-burning, all-purpose kitchen range—just close enough to warm the slowly rotated nakedness without getting a circular brand on the goose-pimpled posterior.

A visit to the "bathroom" was demanding at best, summer or winter. The family dwelling was facetiously referred to as "two bedrooms and a *path*." Anyone venturing out in the dead of winter needed full dress regalia, even a cumbersome overcoat. And, oh, the torture of the seating arrangement! Imagine cold planking treated to months of zero-like weather. I don't think you need be informed that the place seldom doubled as a library.

This particular day had started out almost like any other wintry morning on the "Landbank" place. (Landbank "owned" most of the local farms. The reason for this strange arrangement was far beyond the concept of a preteen during the depths of the Great Depression.) But this day was different in that Dad was gone and it was my turn to assume his chores. Grandma had died and Dad had to travel a considerable distance to take care of her burial, and he had left the responsibilities of the daily farm chores to us boys—my older twin brothers, Ernie and Gene, and me. We shared the morning chores of milking cows, pitching hay from the stuffy mow, feeding horses, slopping hogs and shoveling manure. But we rotated the rest of the farm work between us.

"Son, it's your day to be the man of this house," Mother casually prompted as we sat down to breakfast. I had mixed emotions about the task ahead. Even though it was a happy day of freedom from school I knew the responsibilities of doing Dad's work were pretty demanding even for the hardiest of rugged farm boys.

After a simple prayer of thanksgiving and an earnest petition for safety we quietly ate our meager breakfast of baking powder biscuits, fried cornmeal mush, and cocoa.

"Tell the teacher why I ain't in school today," I called to the twins as they moved out into the frosty mist of a subzero, midwinter morning.

"We will . . . and you be careful," they responded patronizingly as they trudged off through the soft fluff of knee-deep snow. Ernie and Gene were six years older than I.

Be careful? What do they think I am? Some silly kid that can't handle a man's job? I've done these chores so often I could do them with my eyes closed.

"Up and at 'em," Mother chortled.

Oh, how we loved this woman. She had strength of character beyond description. I never knew there were so many proverbs. It seemed like there was one for every day of the year and a few left over for extras on Sunday. Mother was a woman whose children would indeed "rise up and call her blessed" and, of course, "her husband too." Her slightest admonition was a mobilizing command to send a young lad out to take on the most adverse elements.

After I struggled into several layers of clothes from long johns to overalls, I stepped out into the minus-20-degree weather. The chilling cold seared my nostrils and stung my warm cheeks. The elements are the enemy on a farm. An enemy to be feared and respected. In spite of my earlier bravado I quietly admitted to myself that I had better be careful.

The primary task of the day was watering the stock. Particular care was required with the cows. It doesn't take 20-below weather long to freeze those milk-producing faucets. One frosted teat could work a real hardship on a cow, as well as have an adverse effect on the only cash income product at that time of the year.

Arriving at the pump I discovered that the blamed thing was frozen solid and without prospect of producing a drop of water. "No water, no milk," I reasoned simplistically. Some "down on the farm" ingenuity was required here. An obvious solution dawned instantly—remove a couple of the planks from the well platform, bring out one cow at a time, and bail a drink for the old girl with a bucket suspended on a long rope.

"Why, this is easy as shootin' fish in a barrel," I mused as I straddled the gaping hole. The work progressed routinely for an hour or so. Thoughts of warm southern spring breezes filtered through my mind. The warm comfort of the kitchen range beckoned invitingly and caution seemed to drift off with the wind.

An alert observer would have noticed that each pail of

water I drew from below the frost line dribbled water across the planks I stood on, forming a thin coating of ice.

Old Brindle was just about satisfied and she looked up and "smiled" appreciatively. I acknowledged the animal's peculiar effort to communicate and shifted my weight. Then without warning I began slipping awkwardly, first one foot and then the other. I felt a solid blow to my right hip and then a smashing thud to my left shoulder and I was falling free to certain death. "Oh, God," I prayed, "this is it!"

Momentarily stunned as I hit the water, I soon realized that I was still alive and breathing. My first reaction was to call for help. Weighed down by heavy boots and layers of clothing I thrashed violently to stay afloat while screaming hysterically toward the opening far overhead.

Collecting my thoughts, I realized the futility of calling for help. There was no help. So I began to search for a way out. It soon became evident that Dad's crude construction and nature's careful placement of knotholes could serve as a "ladder" to freedom from this would-be watery grave. Slowly, laboriously, and with painstaking deliberation I inched my way upward. Arriving at the top, I discovered I had chosen the wrong side. Two feet of ceiling extended back out over my head—over the water.

Nearly exhausted I calculated one possible chance. Hanging on precariously by the fingertips of one hand, with my toes slotted clumsily in the cracks, I reached out toward the icy ledge that had so treacherously betrayed me only moments before. Grasping the lip with my one free hand and taking a deep breath, I whispered, "Please, please, let me hang on—please!"

With that I swung precipitously for one eternal moment over the icy depths, clinging to the ledge with four frigid fingertips. I grabbed the ledge with my other hand and began a very careful chin-up to the platform level. Slowly I inched my aching, freezing body upward and over. I was free at last.

With a prayer of thanksgiving on my lips I stumbled

awkwardly toward the house. I must have presented a dreadfully shocking sight to Mother as she looked up from her mending to view this frozen spectre that appeared to be her son.

Mother was a strong woman. Her mission in life was to pass her uncommon fortitude on to others—especially to her own. She helped me dress in fresh clothing and warmed my insides with leftover breakfast cocoa, then sent me back out into the cold.

Today I was the man of the house.

The stifling hot July morning smothered the landscape. A lonely hawk drifted silently in quest of unwary field mice. Tiny tufts of cottonwood down drifted lazily to earth. Barnyard fowl in dusty little cloisters scratched the thirsty soil.

There was little mischief available to a tiny five-year-old, but the search continued endlessly. Occasionally there was a call for little hands and feet to marshal forces with the big people in the never-ending cycle of rural survival.

"Son, I need you. It's time to take the water to the field," Mother called from the back stoop.

With that the spell was broken and daydreams evaporated into reality. The task was simple—pump a quart of water from the house-side well. This was the well that supplied the household needs. The barnyard well was far from the house; its water was unfit for people to drink. The barnyard well was the one that nearly provided my personal "Waterloo" some years later.

Pumping from the old well was always a curious event for an inquisitive youngster. Of particular interest was the family of frogs that had taken up residence in its cool recesses. A screen net covering the bottom of the pipe kept the younger members of the frog family out of the pipe and the water bucket. Pouring from a reserve pail into the pump head served to prime the contraption. Reaching high with both arms I hauled on the handle with rapid repetition until cool water spilled plentifully from the spout.

With the fragile jar of water carefully wrapped in a grocery sack I began my slow trek to the cornfield on the hill. Trudging down the lane my bare feet picked their way carefully through ruts sculptured by the spring rains. Lazy cattle huddled stoically in the meager shade of sagging willows, eyes weeping balefully, tails swishing the relentless flies.

The young corn plants, barely a foot high, seemed to sense that summer at that latitude provided a limited growing season. Their green leaves straining from the stalk seemed to wave merrily at soft white moths and darting dragonflies. As a child of five I couldn't quite comprehend that "only God can make a tree" or pussy willows or caterpillars or even make the corn to grow.

Seated upon a rock I placed my valued cargo in the shade of a nearby fence post. The huge team of horses drawing the single-row cultivator lumbered heavily toward me. The jangle of the harness trappings, the snorting nostrils, and the clanking of the machinery created a cacophony of sound sufficient to send my tiny legs scampering several corn rows away.

My brother Gene brought the lumbering animals to a halt with a firm tug on the reins and the customary "Whoa!" The big brother was an object of my keen admiration. I envied his ability to control both animal and machine with such confidence. Especially those animals. I had been present when they were unloaded at the railroad siding. They had just endured the long trip directly from the freedom of the plains of eastern Montana. Snorting loudly, bucking wildly, they had strained at the ropes that tethered them. The wildly flashing eyeballs struck terror in my young heart.

That had been in early spring. By now the dapple gray and the black had been broken and were now redeeming a portion of the 10 dollar purchase price.

I inched cautiously forward with the water. Gene tied

the reins tightly to a convenient lever on the machine. His tired frame slouched wearily in the quack grass near the rocks that laced the fence rows around each field of the home place. Much later I was to learn that those stones were mute evidence that a glacier had once retreated from this land. My dad and brothers had spent untold hours of back-breaking work moving them from the furrow to the fence lines.

After Gene took several deep, satisfying swallows of the tepid water it was time to resume plowing corn. My big brother, always concerned for my welfare, knew well the boredom of hot summer days. Why not give the little guy a ride? Just one round. Down and back. Nothing very exotic, but at least it would help break the monotony of an otherwise humdrum day.

The single-row, horse-drawn cultivator was designed for one operator and no passenger. A little imagination would be required. A small tool box had been mounted on the tongue of the machine directly over the doubletree. Since it was the only flat spot other than the driver's seat, why not perch there, be it ever so precarious.

The bridle-bit pressure released as the reins were relaxed and the animals surged forward with a methodical plodding gait. The view from the tool box was an entirely new experience. My tiny frame was dwarfed by the monstrous haunches. Harness-wear tugged steadily at the singletrees on each side of me. Eight chisel-like shovels plowed the soil, four to each side of the row, deftly, swiftly uprooting the growth that sought to choke the life from the young corn.

My heart beat furiously at the excitement of this new adventure. Not everybody's big brother would take the trouble to give a little brother this kind of ride. We must have made an unlikely sight, bouncing along the first 80 rods. Just one turnaround and back and it would be over. The excitement was paralyzing!

The turnabout was always cumbersome for the horses. They were required to step unnaturally in crossfooted fashion while negotiating the turn. However, they had made the turnaround hundreds of times successfully.

As the bit cut sharply at the corners of their mouths, the spirited animals tossed their heads nervously. The arduous maneuver began. The heavy, lathered bodies bumped and jostled in ungainly fashion as extra stress was placed on the raw piece of green oak that served as a tongue to which the horses were teamed by the neckyoke.

A resounding crack rang out! Like the report from a small-caliber rifle. As the frightened horses bolted into an immediate gallop, my brother catapulted heels-over-head backward from the driver's seat. The near-wild animals ran on at breakneck speed. The most dreaded occurrence of the summer season, apart from a tornado, was happening. Runaway!

It's difficult to accurately describe those next few moments. Quickly losing my grip on my tenuous perch I catapulted headlong into the jaws of that monstrous machine. Eight razor-sharp wedges of cold steel leaped and jerked, alternately digging into the soil and flashing menacingly in the brilliant sunshine. Any one of those devilish blades could have speared me at any moment during their satanic dance.

How I escaped certain death will always remain a mystery. It was as though some prehistoric monster had tried to swallow me and, finding me indigestible, spat me out on the ground. The horses raced across the field to the fence line and then turned toward the barn. As they pulled the cultivator alongside the fence, one wheel of the machine bounced crazily along the rock row for most of a quarter of a mile before the broncos were cornered by the barnyard enclosure. The machine was a total loss and Dad sold it to traveling gypsies.

Gene raced frantically towards the fallen lump partially hidden behind the corn rows. He cried out hysterically in anguish, knowing in his heart that there was no way his brother could have escaped certain death. He knelt over me, a soft moan escaping from his throat. How would he tell Dad and Mom? How could he have used such bad judgment? Of course he knew those broncos were only half broken. Overwhelming distress seemed to consume his spirit.

As he bent to lift my lifeless form he was startled to hear a muffled whimper. To his joy and amazement I appeared to be in one piece and alive! Tenderly he gathered me in his arms and carried me to the house, thinking the worst, praying for the best. There was no hysteria as he laid me gently on the kitchen table for Mother to examine. Her deft fingers exploring expertly soon concluded that the only damage could be treated with a dab of iodine. That was the most painful part of the entire ordeal. Today I wear a fine, white line on my left shoulder blade to remind me of that grim skirmish with what some would be inclined to call fate.

Deep in my heart I knew it was more than fate.

It was little wonder that my godly parents daily petitioned the heavenly Father on behalf of their six children, especially for me, their youngest, although the perils of childhood did not always strike with such dramatic suddenness.

My first grade in school was spent at old District 44, a simple, stark-white, one-room building accommodating eight grades. Even at that early age I was quick to sense that being the only one in my grade certainly left much to be desired. Happily, I absorbed enough by osmosis to be promoted.

Next year I would go to the big school in town which meant that I would have to walk more than three miles each way to school. That may sound like a long hike for second-grade legs, but I had already been conditioned for it. It was the family custom to make the weekly journey to town for church on Sunday morning. Most of the time we walked—in 1932 the automobile was a scarce curiosity in our neighborhood. Occasionally we were treated to a ride in the wagon or sled as the season required.

I didn't especially care to walk that far to sit motionless for an hour or more on those rock-hard benches while the old parson droned through his endless text. I don't remember much of what transpired in those services, but a few things have remained fixed in my memory.

Dad was the strongest man I'd ever known. No boy ever idolized his dad more than I. Who wouldn't admire the strongest, quickest, cleverest, wittiest, happiest man in the whole wide world? But there was one thing that appeared to contradict the image. I had seen my dad cry. Not once, but many times.

Even a seven-year-old knows that a grown man doesn't cry, no matter what the circumstances. And a man certainly doesn't show off his "weakness" in a public place, especially in the church sanctuary. Because I tended to fidget and squirm I usually wound up pretty close to Dad's hip pocket during the worship service. Imagine my consternation the first time I noticed that the big man was weeping silently, seemingly without provocation. Mortifying, absolutely mortifying! There was no place I could hide.

It was many years before I understood that really strong men cry—that strong men sometimes revere God so deeply that tears are the only expression available to them. My dad was the strongest man I ever knew.

Summer wilted like yesterday's blossom. The fall days passed hurriedly through balmy afternoons of Indian summer. Weeping gray skies of early November blended slowly with the onset of winter. Having been stripped naked by the early frosts of autumn, the elm, oak, poplar, and willow stood shivering on the dreary landscape. Night would fall with a spooky suddenness.

More than one afternoon ended abruptly before I reached the little house so far from town. When that happened, the road became a long, sinister hall of darkness. Mysterious sounds of unknown origin reverberated down through the creek bottom and up the hill. Grotesque arms of aging trees reached menacingly out of the dark. My little heart would pound as terror gripped me. Sometimes I whistled and moved on bravely. Then again I would hold my breath and steal ever so softly through the heavy gravel underfoot. On those occasions the lights of home were a welcome sight. It was my first great lesson as to what it really meant to step "from darkness into light."

Some nights I never reached home. It was not at all uncommon to have a blizzard scream in from the northwest, making travel for a fellow of my stature virtually impossible. My 42-inch frame, though draped with nearly 50 pounds of raw muscle, was no match for six-foot drifts and winds gusting to gale-like force.

On those nights I slept in the back room at Emil Splitstoesser's gas station, in the upper bunk. A piece of dry bread and a length of stale sausage served as supper. Homework became a game of checkers with old Emil and bedtime was a bit more tardy than usual. My older brothers usually braved the storm and carried the message home that little brother couldn't make it all the way. Those episodes were not frequent. Usually I ventured out from school about an hour before darkness set in, enough time to reach home just before the blanket of darkness dropped silently.

One day as I left school the low overcast indicated that sunset would start early. The first 3,960 steps were relatively uneventful apart from an unusual snappiness in the air. It was 18 degrees below zero and there was a stiff breeze from the southwest. After that first mile and a half I was chilled to the bone and I decided to turn off the road into the McMartin place. After a few minutes by the fire and a warm drink my strength was renewed. If I was going to make it home by nightfall I had better hustle.

Back on the road I pressed into a headwind. I soon became alarmed to find the drifting snow made walking somewhat near impossible. Better hurry. I struggled on. I had heard those terrifying stories about grown men freezing to death a few feet from safety when wind and snow and darkness blended the landscape into a nothingness, similar to a fog at sea.

Staring straight ahead I was horrified to discover that

my road had disappeared into a "white-out," the most feared of winter's many faces. *Go easy now*, I thought to myself. *Easy does it*, as Dad would say. Checking my bearings I spotted a post from the fence row paralleling the road. Following that fence had to lead me to the next homestead. The snow along the fence was more than waist deep to me, and every step became increasingly difficult. Darkness was falling rapidly. I became painfully aware that I was not physically able to endure much more of the wind and cold and snow.

"God, I don't think I can make it. Will you help me?" Having asked God, it didn't seem proper to spend a lot of time begging. Better to give some feet to that prayer and press on. I knew I could never make it home. If I could just reach the next farm.

What's this? "Whoopee!" The next post wasn't just a post. It was a mailbox by the side of the road. It belonged to another McMartin, but I didn't really care who it belonged to. A few feet further I knew there would be a hedgerow. Follow that hedge to the break and a house would be there.

Gathering my last reserve of strength I stumbled numbly toward the house. I desperately wanted to cry but I resisted that temptation in the interest of my family reputation. Rapping furiously on the door, I waited breathlessly. *What if they aren't home*, I agonized. There was no response. I beat on the door again and waited in despair. Just then the knob turned and the door flung open. What a sight I must have presented. Numb and exhausted, I stepped inside and sank to the floor. I was safe at last.

It was now dark. A mile and a half further down the road a quiet conversation around the dinner table centered on the whereabouts of the youngest member of the family. Had anyone seen me? Had I stayed in town? What if I was still out there in the night? A quiet calm prevailed. No cause for panic. A deep peace enveloped the atmosphere.

All is well. Thank you, God.

My parents really believed! They really believed.

Chapter 2
"Please, Let Me Die"

The door of the ambulance slammed shut. The siren growled angrily as the wagon entered the traffic lane headed toward the big hospital in Chicago. Little did I realize that it would be 26 long, lonely months before I would be home.

The whole episode seemed like some impossible dream, a bizarre nightmare from which I most certainly would soon awaken. Just two or three days before, Coach had called me aside and informed me that I would be starting at right tackle for the opening game of the '46 season for Wheaton College.

"Frost, I think you need to know we're having a few problems at the tackle position and it looks like you'll have to plug the gap for us this week."

Calmly I acknowledged his vote of confidence. Inwardly I was deliriously happy with being named to start. Only six weeks or so earlier Coach Harv barely knew my name. I don't think he was ever aware of the anger that welled up inside me every time I saw him as he dropped by where I was working alongside his number one football recruit during the summer. It seemed to me that his visits were daily, but upon reflection I'm sure my recollection amplified the situation out of proportion.

Nonetheless, each time he called out to Don from the ground below, I silently vowed to crash his football program as a walk-on. I'd show him a thing or two.

Since we were replacing the glass on a greenhouse roof following a devastating hailstorm, more than one wad of putty was hurled in his direction as he drove away. And, fortunately, no one was cut by flying glass from a broken pane which I applied too vigorously in a sudden burst of misplaced energy.

I will make his damed football team. I will, I will! After all, I was six-foot-four-and-a-half, weighed 235 pounds, could run like a young gazelle, and was dumb—so why shouldn't I make a pretty fair football player? Don was only six-foot-three, only weighed 215, could only run like a deer and was probably a whole lot smarter. Now who would you want on your football team?

Making that team was an insufferable process. Football camp with its torturous regimen, the two-a-day practice sessions, the extra effort required just to be noticed, and the desert-like heat of an unseasonal Illinois September all blended into a montage reminiscent of a hitch in the French Foreign Legion.

Don and I were only freshmen and normally freshmen paid their dues, along with 30 or more other aspiring footballers, on the junior varsity "Bombers" for the first year. I wanted no part of that "bomber" crew. It was the big club or bust. And bust I did.

I don't suppose there's a red-blooded, sports-minded kid alive who doesn't aspire to achieve at the professional level. I certainly was no exception. My nights were filled with dreams of "Packers" and "Bears" and "Cardinals." After all, if my coach could coach with George Halas, the original "Papa Bear," couldn't I play for the "Papa Bear" himself?

I had no time to reflect on such mundane things as purposes, priorities or such. Football was God, so get on with the liturgy. Each practice session required me to sacrifice my body, extending it far beyond the normal levels of endurance. I literally tried to hit harder, run faster and go longer than any other member on the team. My first stop after each practice session was usually over a soil basin where I would wretch violently for several moments. Then I'd stagger to a nearby bench, close to total collapse.

I will make his darned team. I will. I will!

Sometimes I would get caught up in a highly inflated concept of my own importance. One particular instance comes vividly to mind. Expectations for the '46 season were unusually high as large numbers of men had returned from military service, I among them. Consequently, the Chicago papers took special notice of the small-time football program that was about to make it big. Numerous reporters and photographers were dispatched to Wheaton to report to the whole world.

Two of us, Chuck and I, were selected for special attention. Chuck was a powerful, hard-running fullback who was eventually to lead Wheaton to national recognition and be named as a small-college All-American. He was also on a number of All-Midwest teams including the major university football powers of that era. I recall being very impatient with the whole process. I'm not sure I even extended the newspaper photographer the courtesy of standing still long enough for him to get his picture. I was just too busy with the business at hand. If he wanted a really good picture of me for the Chicago press, he could come Saturday and get an action shot of this young freshman "phenom" making a devastating tackle or a vicious game-breaking block on some poor, unsuspecting linebacker.

That fellow may have been at Saturday's game. I was not. I was never in a game again.

For several days I had been gently complaining to coaches, trainer or doctor—anyone who would listen. Not too vigorously, you understand; that might jeopardize my newfound glory. Nevertheless I felt obliged to tell them that the aches and pains I was experiencing did not seem to be consistent with those of my teammates.

"You'll be alright."

"Football is a tough game."

"You've been hitting it harder than most of the guys for the past three weeks so you ought to have a little more pain."

"The best way to get rid of the football miseries is to run them off," I was told. So run I did. But the nagging ache did not go away.

Upon arising I felt great, but as the day wore on a nagging headache gnawed at my temples. Running seemed to be more of an effort than ever before and by nightfall a mild temperature left me feeling cold and clammy. This went on for several days. One day I said, "Why don't I stop at the infirmary and check with the Doc?"

The doctor was unconcerned. "You have a temp of 99.8. Take a couple of aspirin, drink a lot of water, get a good night's sleep and you'll be fine."

About noon the next day I was sitting in "Prexy's" Western civilization class, one of my favorites. Yesterday's gnawing headache had become a pounding sledgehammer. Ordinarily I would have stuck it out until class dismissal, but that day I leaned over and whispered into a classmate's ear, "Would you mind walking to the infirmary with me? I don't feel too good."

The nurse placed the back of her hand to my forehead and agreed that I might have a fever. Moments later, after reading the thermometer, she beckoned me to follow her to a room down the hall. There she handed me a hospital gown and suggested that I might want to stay the rest of the day since my temp was in excess of 104 degrees. That sounded like a reasonable idea, so I stayed.

I really didn't like the idea of missing football practice one bit but I soon fell into an exhausted sleep and didn't awaken until Doc came in after practice. His immediate diagnosis was flu.

About midnight I awoke in a cold sweat. I felt some sense of alarm but was comforted by the presence of the duty nurse and the antiseptic protection of the environment. A sudden wave of nausea prompted me to get to my feet and grope my way down the hall to the washroom. As I bent wearily over the basin I suddenly crashed clumsily to the floor.

Addressing myself harshly I thought, *How stupid of you! Can't you even stand on your own two feet anymore?*

I reached for the nearest plumbing fixture to help lift myself into a standing position, intending to return to my room. How strange. I couldn't seem to get my legs in the right position to accomplish that simple act. I felt so foolish and was reluctant to call for help. But no matter how I tried I could not get to my feet.

It struck me with brutal suddenness. *I can't stand on my own two feet anymore!*

The next morning—Friday—a host of grim-faced doctors and nurses stood around my bed, muttering in muted tones and glancing furtively at one another as they joined, in deadly earnest, in playing the age-old game of "Diagnosis, diagnosis, who has the diagnosis?"

The rhythmic hum of the tires served to lull my consciousness into a near state of limbo. I had little comprehension of what was really happening. How could I be walking Wednesday and within 48 hours be completely paralyzed from the waist down? *Where were they taking me? Who would be starting at tackle for today's game? Why must I be taken to Chicago to be hospitalized?* I wondered if this would be a passing episode of short duration. *Why me? How would I keep up with my class work? When would I get to assemble my new Harley Davidson that was still in the crate? My . . . me . . . mine . . . I . . .*

I was jolted from my introspection by the sudden braking of the ambulance at the loading dock. White-clad orderlies lifted the gurney roughly to the ground. Quickly they wheeled their cargo to a waiting elevator, entered, then exited on the third floor. If I had had a clue as to what I was to experience in the next 13 days I think I would have asked to be deposited in the elevator shaft and forgotten.

This hospital may not have been Chicago's finest hospital, but it was the largest. The summer of '46 had been a disease disaster. Hundreds of thousands had been struck down by the then incurable, dreaded scourge—infantile paralysis. Since hospitals everywhere were filled beyond capacity, I was destined for this place. I was not sure whether I had been admitted or committed.

My bed, a relic retrieved from the Spanish-American War, faced away from the window. Black soot cloaked the vaulted ceiling. Two monstrous eye-like globes peered menacingly from the blackness. Some years before, someone had washed as high as he could reach from the floor. When he stopped he left a macabre decorative effect of a dusky drop ceiling against pallid walls.

The eight-bed ward was populated by seven wildly maniacal, screaming children between the ages of 2 and 10. I was reminded of the little Sunday School ditty, "Red and yellow, black and white, all are precious in His sight." Well, I wasn't quite sure He was anywhere about, and the little "darlings" were anything but precious. Why the little tyrants hadn't been discharged to make room for some really sick people was beyond me.

Settling into my new environs I began to perceive current medical practice as something of a medieval art. Much of my recollection of those days has been graciously hazed as a cloudy memory. I had some strange notion that when I got to the hospital, doctors would swarm around my bed, dutifully attended by angels in white. Samples of blood, bowel and bladder would be rushed to gleaming laboratories for instant analysis. Diagnosis would be immediate. The prognosis would be positive and swift. Recovery would be rapid and complete. *Hey, I'm almost well!*

Be careful now, this is no time for hysteria.

However, time ground to a halt. Instead of a doctor, an attendant in street clothes silently attached an identification to the foot of the bed.

NAME: FROST, WALLACE E.
AGE: 19   RACE: CAUCASIAN
RELIGION: PROTESTANT
DIAGNOSIS: UNKNOWN
SPECIAL ORDERS: NO AMBULATION

The hours dragged on and I could feel the first major crisis beginning to build. At first I called gently for some assistance. Whether I could not be heard because of the din created by my ward-mates or because the nurses' station was too distant, I do not know. My repeated calls finally garnered a response. I had been trying for hours to use the urinal but without results.

"I think I need to be catheterized," I said.

"I'll notify the nurse," came the terse response.

The minutes turned into hours. I don't think you can know how excruciatingly agonizing it is when you have to and can't.

"Can't you do something? I'm desperate," I cried.

"But there are no orders."

It had now been some 14 hours. I sobbed softly in my pillow, chewing viciously at the corner of the sheet. Being unable to turn over by myself, two student nurses had tenderly turned me on my side. Still no orders, no nurses, no relief. The ward lights were out. The children slept.

Lord, something's got to give. It's just got to. It just has to . . .

A soft hand brushed a tear from my cheek. "It's OK," she said. "It will only take a minute to mop the floor and—and I'm so relieved for you."

Her tender touch was one of the few pleasant memories of that place.

It had been nearly 24 hours since I'd slept. Sheer exhaustion numbed my consciousness. At last—sleep.

I was awakened harshly as those monstrous lights blazed overhead. The stark reality of a new day pierced the veil and I surveyed my prison. This was decision day. No one had yet ventured a diagnosis. The needle had been withdrawn from the crook in my elbow. The antibody serum had apparently been less than effective. Laboratory analysis of spinal fluid had served only to add to the confusion.

"It's not readily determinable what has caused your condition. We will order the Sister Kenny treatment."

With that limited explanation the doctors moved on. After all, there were many to see since the place was operating at a 110-percent capacity. And since there were thousands upon thousands of cases of polio that summer, was it not reasonable to assume that all the patients had it?

I had heard about this wonderful miracle-working process imported from "down under." Somewhere I had read that hot packs were applied to immobile limbs continually around the clock. The immediate effect was to comfort tender muscles. The long-term response to the therapy was the restoration of mobility. Oh, it all sounded so wonderful! It would be no time at all and I would be rarin' to go. Hey, maybe even before the football season was over!

Unfortunately, the saintly Sister Kenny was not there to supervise the application to my case. I'm not too certain just what orders the doctor left but I was later to wish with all my heart that he had left no orders at all. The initial wrap with the pack, blisteringly hot, did soothe the aching muscles. But it wasn't long until all the warmth dissipated and I was left for hours to lie in that soggy, cold flannel until I fairly shivered with the chill. No amount of pleading or cajoling brought relief. I simply waited miserably until the "rag wrappers" made their next rounds. I don't believe they ever managed to make the change more than three or four times in a day. Surely this was not what that Kenny lady really intended.

The days wore on and the pain ripened. Only with the most careful effort could I be turned without excruciatingly painful results. My once sinewy, rugged muscles refused to tolerate the slightest touch, and helping hands dared to hold my lifeless limbs only by the bony protrusion at the joints. Occasionally a well-intentioned aid would forget and grip me firmly by one calf, which called a howl of agony from my lips.

Since the pain was so unrelenting, sleep became a precious commodity. My body seldom surrendered until three or four in the morning. Repeated requests for something to dull the symptoms fell on deaf, unbelieving ears.

"Polio doesn't yield the kind of pain you claim you have. You must be imagining it. I will order 10 grains of aspirin [two] for sleep."

The result was obvious. Sleep was only occasional and of the briefest duration. Since the entire building was under quarantine, everyone except authorized personnel was kept out. I can't recall even seeing a doctor more than three or four times during those interminable 13 days. An austere nurse passed through sometime during the morning hours. The timeless monotony of the days and endless nights were infrequently interrupted by orderlies and student nurses carrying out the minimal requirements of hospital survival.

I had heard horror stories in the past about this vermin- and rodent-ridden excuse for a hospital. One family friend had shared the experience of their preschool child who also had been "incarcerated" in the communicable disease section. For months afterward she awakened with nightmarish screams, imagining that the rodents, the roof-rats, were again visiting her bed. To this day I'm grateful that I did not experience a similar visitation.

The place was something less than antiseptic. The floor was scrubbed but unpolished. The sooty ceiling hung like a gloomy cloud of oppression. The pasty grey walls seemed to carry the pallid complexion of an incurable sickness. Broken ceiling plaster threatened to fall on my head. Unwashed window panes could have served aptly in a cathedral of death.

Death! Suddenly a fascinating prospect.

But not just now. Although the rodents failed to appear, another form of pest was having a field day. And I was the field! At first I brushed frantically, knocking them to the floor. But in the quiet darkness of the witching hour they moved in relentlessly. Since I couldn't prevent their encroachment upon my person, I determined I would fight back with a dogged determination. Much of the time I laid on my back in the darkness, my feverish skin exposed to the waist. Silently but certainly the multilegged creatures would crawl up the bed post and then venture up and across my bare chest. Patiently I waited, carefully plotting the course and speed of the unseen intruder. At just the right moment I slapped viciously, crushing the pesky creature to death. Warily I picked it up and placed it carefully on the bedside stand.

At dawn's earliest light their bravado faded rapidly and they disappeared through the crevices from whence they came. Before there was a stirring in the ward I cautiously examined my night's achievement. *Wow! Nine! Nine huge cockroaches! A night's work to be proud of,* I thought. I cannot describe my disappointment when the char-woman, while making her early refuse round, simply swept the evidence of my triumph into her bucket. Not even a courteous, "Congratulations."

Had I not been seeking some measure of claim to fame? This was it! More cockroaches killed on a bare chest in bed in one night than ever recorded before! It would prove interesting in the years ahead to challenge any and all as to who had killed more.

As the days wore on, the magnitude of my plight began to weigh heavily on my tortured mind and body. Where would it all end? The questions began to multiply in a geometric progression. And answers? There were no answers. I had been defeated. Disease had prevailed and won. Death seemed to beckon with cunning craftiness.

I had thought for years that God and I had been on good terms. Not that I had been any saint, you under-stand, but certainly I had made some vows and paid the minimal dues. That should have been enough to buy a little insurance for my physical well-being. Surely it de-served better than this! As I wallowed like a slothful hog in the mire of self-pity, the pain, the discouragement, the desperation, the despair and the seemingly abject destitution drove me to the very brink of my sanity. I reasoned this way: *If I could never walk again, never run, never climb, never play tennis or handball or golf or basketball or baseball, or never wrestle or swim or cycle or, above all, never play football again, what was the use of carrying on at all? Wouldn't I be better off, well, you know better off, uhhh, better off not being?*

Now, that was a worthy thought. Just sidestep outside through the back door of life and call it quits. No more pain, no tears, no long years of invalidism. No burden to society and family. Most of all, no mental anguish of watching others and not . . . Even though the idea of ending it all seemed to have a great deal of merit I surely couldn't get the job done on my own. I needed help.

During the Big War, the number II version, it became pretty well accepted that there was a believer in every foxhole. Well, I was in the deepest foxhole a guy could be in. I would appeal to the same court to which all those other fellows had gone. It's easy to pray when the chips are down. Mine was a simple prayer.

Lord, you know how bad I want to get out of this fix I'm in. I'm hurtin' all over and can't get no pills for the pain. I've always been doin' things that were fun—especially games and stuff. It doesn't look like there is much hope that I'll ever play those games again.

I'm sick and tired and discouraged and depressed. It don't look like it's gonna get any better. So, God, the next time I fall asleep, please don't let me wake up. Please, please let me die.

Chapter 3
No Longer Lonely

The social worker brought the best news I had received so far. The doctor who had committed me to this ugly refuge had made a big mistake. I should never have been sent here at all. "You will be transferred to the veterans hospital at Hines the first thing in the morning."

Deliverance at last.

Moments after being transferred from the litter to the bed by the ambulance attendants, an angel in white jabbed a hypodermic needle deep into my buttocks. In a matter of minutes I slipped softly into a sound sleep that lasted for hours and hours. It was the first relief from pain I had experienced in nearly three weeks. However, pleasant and comfortable as it was, it was just an interlude.

In two days I was transferred to neurology. Most of the patients were three or four times my age and had been the victims of strokes. The medical staff hastily established a regimen of educational and physical therapy for me. There was only one minor problem. The doctor assigned to me had a number of preconceived notions about my case. After all, he had read the chart and the prior diagnosis was polio. Severe pain was not associated with it, so consequently I didn't really hurt. Again, it was just my imagination.

"Shut up and go to sleep, kid." A cantankerous old veteran with a salty mouth expressed his frustration at this intruder who whined and murmured while most of the others slept. There was no way he could understand.

The days wore on, broken regularly by a steady stream of family, friends, and the curious at visiting hours. One really bright spot during the entire rehabilitation process arrived daily by mail. My dear sister Lois managed to drop some bit of communication into the postal box every single day for the entire 795 days of my hospital stay. That singular act of love carried a healing balm far beyond the realm of medical arts.

The first two months at Hines Veterans Hospital I was almost completely bedridden. Thirty minutes of sitting was a laborious effort. In spite of the constant discomfort and the sleepless nights the place seemed like a little bit of heaven on earth compared to the last hospital. There were long hours of reflection and introspection. I struggled intensely with the why of it all. But this was not the first time that I got the feeling that life had somehow passed me by.

One chilly fall morning on the farm in Illinois, Dad had just announced that since all of the boys were grown and leaving the farm, he and Mother would be accepting an assignment with the local state reformatory for boys near Saint Charles, Illinois. They would become surrogate parents for heavy-duty delinquents from throughout the state. On the surface it seemed to be the epitome of social and spiritual consciousness and I instantly glowed with pride. I would be staying behind, in my brothers' care, to go to school. I had been anxious to be a man for some time, and now I'd made it. I'd turned 13 a few days earlier.

I reasoned that any kid alive would be wild with the great prospect of total emancipation at that early juncture in life. Little did I know the future pitfalls. Nor did I recognize that the trauma of those adolescent years would prepare me well for more dire days ahead.

It was little wonder that the wagging tongues of local

gossips summarily determined that I was guilty of every local vice. Their myopic mentalities fabricated enough evidence to hang Bluebeard. Then, having established my guilt beyond a shadow of doubt, they proceeded to convict and whisper judgment all over town. I was never once allowed to take the stand in my own defense.

On the other hand, I can remotely sympathize with their vain imaginations. Had I not lived in several different rooms in the past few months? Rooms? Well, sometimes. More often a basement or an attic. Wasn't I the waif who dusted shelves, washed windows and scrubbed floors at Phil's Haberdashery? Or delivered papers at 4:00 A.M.? Or washed dishes for 14 hours on Saturday in the Main Street Coffee Shop? Perhaps I should have forgiven them sooner. Forgiving seems to come so late.

While I was working in the coffee shop, more than once I had to physically restrain Scott, a college-age coworker. He would protest bitterly, "But can't you see what that dirty pipe layer is doing to that pretty girl in the end booth?" Of course I could see, but it was obvious that she was well paid for the indignities. She wouldn't follow a pipeline crew across the country unless she was.

Red, one of the customers, was a semiprofessional baseball player who could break off one nasty curve but who struck out repeatedly in the game of life. At times his friends would drag him back through the kitchen and down to the basement to sleep off his drunken stupor. Bug-eyed and curious, I pondered the magnitude of his plight. The scene was enacted repeatedly over the years.

One day Red disappeared from the place. Little did I realize that more than 40 years later I would be using Red as a prime example of a man who had really gone into the pit and then miraculously found a way out. He found solid rock and is now a classic example to men everywhere. More about Red later.

One hour in the sink equated to one 30-cent meal. For every meal I didn't eat I collected 25 cents hard cash. Since the cash was always in short supply, I managed to wangle a job at the high school cafeteria. I exchanged one study hall for one lunch period for one lunch.

One day I was called to the principal's office.

"Young man," old M.F. intoned, "we are going to have to suspend you from school indefinitely."

My heart leaped to my throat. "But why, Sir? What have I done that's so bad?"

"You were seen writing your initials on the washroom wall and we simply can't have that."

"But there isn't a guy in school who hasn't left his name or something somewhere around this place," I argued plaintively. "Shouldn't they all be kicked out too?" It never occurred to me that the man wasn't playing it straight.

He went on lecturing me sternly about decency, honesty, citizenship and I don't know what all. All I do know is that it was a brutally dehumanizing experience. It had been strongly ingrained in me from my earliest days that anything done that brought dishonor on the family name was totally unacceptable. And here I was, faced with the most serious discipline the school could muster, seemingly for the most trivial infraction imaginable. With shoulders drooping forlornly, hands plunged deeply into my pockets, I slipped dejectedly from the office. What would I tell Dad and Mom?

It was not until the middle of the next year that I learned from a kindly shop teacher the real reason for the summary dismissal. Someone had been stealing silverware from the school cafeteria. Since all the other kids who worked in the place were from "regular" homes under the supervision of their parents, they had been eliminated as possible suspects. That left me as the only logical possibility. Guilty by inference alone.

Three days after the incident I was readmitted without explanation. It seemed the real culprit had become bolder with his misdeeds and was caught red-handed. I had been secretly pronounced innocent and readmitted without apology for the mistaken identity. M.F. died shortly after that. I wasn't highly motivated to attend the memorial service. I pledged deep within my heart to never ever pronounce judgment without a hearing, especially if the accused was just a kid.

I expected the principal to be an ogre, but surely the teachers were a decent sort. A likeable biology teacher was to prove otherwise. This teacher assigned a project that would take several weeks. The subject was individual choice so I eagerly launched into a thorough investigation of keen interest—pilot training. It seemed as if I spent every free minute reading, observing or interviewing. The local people were helpful, supplying a surplus of information to sift, analyze and refine. From that I was able to prepare a piece of work of which I could be rightfully proud. Even though I didn't know how to type, I punched away at the treatise using the hunt-and-peck method. I was eager to submit it for evaluation, confident that it would rank among the very best.

Friday evening, Marshall, a fine scholar and good friend, called, "Wally, do you have the project finished that is due Monday?"

"Yeah, matter of fact, it is terrific. It's the best thing I've ever done! Why?"

"Well, I, uh, I forgot all about it and I haven't got a thing to hand in. Could I read yours and write about the same subject? I could rough it up enough so 'Teach' would just think it was a coincidence we chose the same subject. How about it, huh?"

There was a long silence on the phone. I knew it was really wrong to deceive our teacher by the proposed subterfuge. On the other hand I didn't really want to leave a friend in the lurch. Oh, why not? I would not be the one cheating, it would be Marshall. "OK," I responded, "you can have it over the weekend but be sure and get it back to me by Sunday night. I'd sure hate to have anyone see you give it to me at school on Monday."

The projects were mostly lengthy and involved. It was nearly two weeks before they were graded and returned. I was secretly curious if anyone besides myself would be getting an *A* grade. Imagine my keen disappointment at seeing a big black *C* written across the title page. Consternation and confusion registered heavily as the dismissal bell sounded. I couldn't wait to compare grades with some of the better students in the class. Particularly, Marshall.

I suspect you may have already guessed. "I got an *A*! What did you get?" he chortled.

I tried to act nonchalant. "Oh, I got a *C*. There must have been a mistake. I'll talk to him tomorrow during his office hours." I was absolutely certain that such a glaring injustice would be righted swiftly.

That night I pondered how I could bring up Marshall's *A* without revealing our mutual complicity with twin subjects. It would be enough to suggest that it was plainly obvious that my work was far superior to his. Shouldn't the grades have simply been reversed?

To this day I don't think the teacher ever suspected the actual chain of events. His words pierced my spirit like a fiery dart. "Your friend wrote a fine paper. It deserved an *A*. Your paper was much better than his. Matter of fact, it was so good that I don't really believe it's yours. I'm convinced that *you must have copied it from someone else*. You're lucky I didn't give you an *F*. I don't want to hear any more about it."

If that's what he wants to believe, let him believe it, I thought. *I'll never betray my friend with further explanation.* Silently I moved out into the hall, permitting him to believe that he was completely justified in his omniscience.

The determination deepened within me. Never pronounce judgment based solely upon a supposition. Every kid deserves a hearing.

Another unforgettable episode took place in my junior literature class. At last I had found a teacher who appreciated me strictly on the basis of my performance. She was objectively aloof from the undeserved reputation that followed me almost everywhere.

While the rest of the students struggled to write a paragraph of acceptable prose during a class period, I frequently was inspired to dash off a flowery bit of verse.

"Genius," she would cry. "This is wonderful. May I read it to my other English classes?"

I would rather she not. I must admit that it was somewhat flattering to be noticed but I would have been much more excited if it had been recognition from the football coach. Her enthusiasm eventually surpassed rational thought. The dear soul's pet project was advising a small group of students organized as the Script Club. I *had* to join.

I couldn't get on the football team because of a minor physical problem, which was bad enough. But to then identify with that bunch of teacher-pet types? I'd be the only one over five-foot-four and the only one who didn't wear glasses. Besides that, they met after school and I worked every night. No, I couldn't be a member. In spite of my protestations she persisted in pressing the issue.

In time, the relationship deteriorated to open hostility. I reasoned that silence would be my best defense. It worked briefly. One day she flung the gauntlet down before the entire class. "Mr. Frost, if you don't start speaking out in class you will receive an *F* in this class."

How preposterous, I thought. *I never get anything less than a B on any of my papers. No way she can give me an F.* With the comfort of that thought reinforcing my abstinence I firmly resolved to call her bluff.

The weeks passed swiftly as the summer recess swung into view. One of the last big moments before pandemonium broke loose with the final dismissal bell was report card distribution. Some of the kids just jammed the whole packet into their pocket and left. It could be pretty deflating to have others see those *D*s and *F*s.

Not so for me. My grades would reflect my best effort. I didn't mind comparing grades with anybody. Or so I thought until my unbelieving eyes fell on that big red *F* in literature.

"She did it! The old bag actually kept her word and did it," I mumbled to myself as I numbly rose from the seat and stumbled robot-like toward the exit. My first impulse was to rush to her room and protest the inequity of it all. "How can you give one of your best English students this kind of a grade just because you're mad at him?" I rehearsed. "But that is exactly what she wants. She would love to see me grovel." She had never been known to change a grade anyway.

I rushed for the exit, leaping down the long stairs several steps at a time. I'd had it. There was no justice to be found in that place. My resolve was ever deeper. Justice must be served. The punishment cannot exceed the infraction. It's particularly important with kids.

Bursting through the door into the brilliant June sunlight I vowed, "I'll never go back!"

I didn't.

A sudden inspiration struck me! One of my brothers, Lyle, an Air Force pilot, had once commented casually, "If there is ever anything I can do for you, just let me know." I hastily drafted a telegram and fired it off to his station in Puerto Rico, a submarine air search unit. "Need year's tuition for senior year at academy. Stop. Can you help? Stop. Explain later. Stop. Gratefully, Wally."

What a year. I thought I had gone to education heaven. The experiences of that year would more than make the subject matter for a book. No one made assumptions about my character based solely on my circumstances. If a problem arose there was always someone to turn a listening ear. If there was an embarrassing moment, it had a humorous side.

An assignment in senior English required the recitation of a selected verse of our choice. At first I thought I'd use something original, but past experiences discouraged that. I decided to stick to something familiar by a well-known author. Ah, I had it! Just the right thing. It would allow for the most effective oral interpretation.

"Wally, will you be the first to recite for us today?" the

teacher inquired kindly. Of course I had practiced diligently. Every inflection and pause was in place. All I had to do was say it like I'd learned it. So with all the feeling I could bring to bear I began "Daffodils," by William Wordsworth.

> I wandered lonely as a cloud
> That floats on high o'er vales
> and hills,
> When all at once I saw a crowd,
> A host, of golden daffodils;
> Beside the lake, beneath the trees,
> Fluttering and dancing in the breeze.

I was never able to finish the first verse in its entirety. Near the end of the second line the whole class was convulsing with laughter, including the prim and proper "Miss English." Repeatedly the class recovered and I was requested to begin anew. The response was the same. Hysterical laughter and tear-stained cheeks.

Watching this bulky, oversized football type interpret sensitive verse with all the airs of Little Lord Fauntleroy was more than they could cope with. I never did finish my recitation. I got an *A.*

What was so different about that year? Why was there such a dramatic change between those first three years of high school and the senior year? *Those people really cared.* They were Christians.

There had been others who cared. There was Uncle Joe, affectionately known by local boys as the founder of a boys' club called Christian Service Brigade. I was constantly amazed how a full-time college student could devote so many countless hours to the needs of boys in that community. It seemed like he never failed me.

I recall one night when I was particularly depressed. It had been more than two weeks since I had been in touch with my parents. I'd just found a new place to room. Well, it wasn't really a room, sort of an attic over a one-story bungalow. Access was by an outside stairway. The only furnishings were a small bureau and a bunk bed. My clothes, hung openly from nails driven into the exposed two-by-fours supporting the roof, cast grotesque shadows at the far end of the cavern-like space. The area was dimly lighted by one 40-watt bulb hanging at the peak of the A-shaped enclosure. It seemed to me that the place was lacking some of the normal comforts of home.

Joe had found me at the Prince Castle or some such eating place. I had eaten a 10-cent lunch—a nickel hamburger and a coke—before heading for "home." He offered me a ride.

As we approached the house the awful fear of spending another night in that place struck me forcefully.

"Joe," I sobbed quietly, "I hate this place. I'm so lonely and scared when I go to bed at night. I can hardly stand it. It's blacker than a coal mine when the light goes out. To tell you the truth, I usually put my head under the covers first and then turn the light out by pulling the long string that hangs down from the ridge pole."

We sat quietly for a few moments.

"No longer lonely, no longer lonely . . ." Joe had begun to sing softly. It was his way. He seemed to always teach with a story or a song. "Why don't you try to sing this song tonight when you turn the light out?" He recited the words and then encouraged me to sing it with him.

> No longer lonely, no longer lonely,
> For Jesus is the Friend of friends to me;
> No longer lonely, no longer lonely
> For Jesus is the Friend of friends to me.[1]

We sang in unison. Softly at first and then with increasing tempo and crescendo we sang.

No one will ever know the comfort imparted to my fearful spirit that night. Jesus cared . . . Joe cared too.

How peacefully I slept.

Another who cared in a very special way was my brother Gene. We had roomed together briefly from time to time over the years. During my senior year in high school, while Gene was at Wheaton College, we stayed in a partially completed building that Dad was constructing on his days off from the reform school.

Winter had come but the insulation hadn't. It was a bit like sleeping in a refrigerator. We turned in unison in bed, so that our bodies contoured continually, thereby conserving as much heat as possible.

The only time sleeping had been colder was in the attic of that little farmhouse in Minnesota in the early thirties. At least here the snow didn't filter through the cracks and form tiny drifts on top of the bed clothing as it did in Minnesota. And we didn't have to make that long run "out back" in the middle of the night. We had *some* of the modern conveniences, just not all.

Since this was the first year I had been free to participate in athletics, Gene was most solicitous of my good health and general well-being. We usually shared one hot meal a day together. More often than not it was a one-dish affair prepared in an old skillet over a wood-burning stove—potatoes, onions, eggs and almost any available vegetables all stirred together. The rest of our meals were cold cereal and equally cold sandwiches.

Now a buck was not easy to come by in those days. My working hours had been curtailed because of football, basketball and the like. My budget was a day-to-day affair and I knew that Gene's was even more severe.

I shall never forget the night when he approached me awkwardly about how I was feeling and how basketball was going. "I think you should have more than one hot meal a day if you're going to do your best. Here is ten bucks I got from Dad for tuition but I want you to have it. I can get along OK without it."

Wow! I was speechless. That would buy me a hot lunch for nearly two months. I must have muttered, "Thanks." I don't recall. But I will always remember that sacrificial act of love and giving.

Someone has said, "Living is giving." My brother

Gene knew something about living.

The heavy snoring of sleeping hemiplegics brought me back to the reality of the moment. It was now after 2:00 A.M. Today I would visit the psychiatrist. My doctor repeatedly insisted that my pain was not real. I had been a medic in the service and we had lots of those kinds of patients in the ward where I worked as a neuropsychiatric technician. If the pain was imagined it was called "psychosomatic." Well, if I was a psycho I wanted to know about it. Better yet, let him talk me out of it. Reluctantly the doctor had made me a "shrink" appointment for the next morning.

The session went well. Before we finished, the psychiatrist made the unprofessional suggestion that maybe it was my doctor who should have had the appointment. "You are perfectly sane. The pain is real. I am writing you a prescription for 100 mgs. of sodium amytal, effective tonight. We are going to get you some rest for a change." That night I slept like a baby. The second good night's sleep in nearly six weeks.

It had been a strange coincidence. The psychiatrist's office was in the very building where I had served in the military. What an experience that was! We were assigned to the lock-up ward for 12 hours a day, six-and-a-half days a week. The average stay for a corpsman on that ward was only seven or eight weeks. It was either move on or become a serious candidate to check in, but without a key.

What a dreadful memory. If I thought I was having a bad time of it now, I was infinitely better off than those poor wretches. There was Greg, a beautiful physical specimen at 20 years. He sat and stared most of his waking hours. Clenching and unclenching his fists ceaselessly. Frequently breaking into uncontrolled sobbing. The ear-shattering scream of German eighty-eights echoed to the deepest recess of his being. There was not a mark on him but he was as surely destroyed as if one of those shells had burst within his bowels.

Leonard was a "hill man" from Tennessee. He had left

his wife Marla and his eight children to enlist in the army. It was scant weeks before he was exchanging fire with the Japanese in the steaming jungles of Guadalcanal. He had never heard of battle fatigue, but now he was a victim. "Battle fatigue" apparently took in the entire spectrum of psychiatric nomenclature. Len was a raging bull, almost continually in a manic state.

One night about 2:00 A.M. several of us had secured him in the tub. Heavy canvas held him firmly under water with just his head protruding. Rapidly fluctuating water temperatures usually had a tranquilizing effect, leaving the patient totally exhausted. That night it didn't work and I was locked in the tub room with him.

From his special vantage point in the hammock he "saw God" coming to deliver him. The purpose in delivering him was to "free me to kill you," he roared. By the time I was able to fumble the key into the lock he had literally ripped his way free through the rugged canvas cover. I had escaped by a hair's breadth. After that Len was never alone with one man.

Lefty, my co-worker in the psychiatric ward, and I had volunteered repeatedly for overseas duty. We reasoned that being a battlefield medic would be better than this. However, the shortage of psych-techs was even greater than field types, so there we stayed—for nearly two years. We had obviously lost any chance for a purple heart. That didn't mean we couldn't shed a little blood.

The mornings we teamed with Dr. Hargrove administering electro-shock therapy were relatively uneventful. We had developed the procedure to a refined science. The alternate days of insulin sub-shock were usually chaotic. With 20 patients on the verge of grand mal seizures we rushed from bed to bed with sugar-saturated orange juice to stem the reaction to the medication. Occasionally we miscalculated or were just plain late.

A grand mal episode was in full bloom in bed three. An immediate injection of glucose was our only recourse. I was pretty good with the needle but because of my size and wrestling experience I was frequently a "holder." One man grabbed the patient's legs, and I applied a double wrist lock to his arm, but no one grabbed his head. That rascal bit all the way through my white jacket, my shirt and my undershirt into my shoulder. I couldn't let go or his arm would flex and likely break the needle off in his vein. I howled with pain.

And the man had syphilis! *Oh Lord,* I thought, *now I've got it too.*

I would get no purple heart but would bear the scar as a remembrance the rest of my days. Later I wrote some poetry in memory of those poor fellows.

The Aftermath

Bold, bleak, barren haunting walls
Encaptured tired, witless men
Whose thoughts and acts betray the stress
The horrors of war attribute them.

Men dead to kindness, love, or pain,
Who walk the floor with aimless tread,
Engulfed in nothingness and woe,
From them all hope or joy has fled.

Men fleeing haunting voice and noise.
Alas, no refuge for them here,
Resigned, themselves to grief and sorrow,
A living hell for them to fear.

They care for naught—request no favor,
Expecting but a meager portion
Of what frugal means there is to offer,
Displaying dull or lost emotion.

They sit through stuporous waning hours.
A Soul bending beneath the burden,
Desiring only that some ministering angel

Might draw the final curtain.

What manner of fate has stricken these
To nigh inanimation,
Disrupting that of Nature's best,
The pride of God's creation?

God scourge the lords who thrive on war,
Who profit at a cost
Of broken, useless, shapeless men,
The mind or life that's lost.

May He grant mercy to these men
Who've paid a price so great,
Restore them by His gracious favor,
Unleash them from such cruel fate.

Note

1. "No Longer Lonely" by Robert Harkness. Broadman Press, Owner.

Chapter 4
Romantically Speaking

"If you can extend your sit-up endurance to one hour you may go home for Thanksgiving Day."

Believe me, I took the bait. Sitting for just a few minutes was an ordeal but it was a welcome change from nearly two months of "flat out." Each day I determined to stick to it a few more minutes. Biting my lip, I literally sweat it out. The excitement of the prospect of a day pass was a tremendous incentive. I wanted it in the worst way.

My brother Lyle arrived promptly at 12:00 and helped me into my civies. It was a cold, blustery, overcast afternoon requiring plenty of wraps. Somehow it seemed just the way a Thanksgiving morning in the Midwest should be.

Every move was ever so gentle. Cautiously we made our way out of the big, red brick building and into the face of a stiff breeze. I began to wonder if I was really ready for this. The comfort and warmth of the ward suddenly seemed to be very attractive. Making the transfer from the hospital bed to a wheelchair was no mean task, but making it from the chair to the car seat was something else. We managed.

Thanksgiving dinner was to be at my sister Maryann's. Most of the family would be present and expectation was keen. The welcome was as cordial as the situation would allow. Maryann's sons, David, Phillip, and Paul, all under five, were bug-eyed with curiosity at the gaunt specter of their Uncle Wally arriving in a wheelchair. There was little time for ceremony. I was nearly exhausted and needed to stretch out on the couch. At dinner I was again propped in my chair. Heads bowed quietly. Dad prayed. It was truly a genuine prayer of thanksgiving.

I don't recall all the details of the day, but one recollection stands out vividly. One guest had been invited who was not a member of the immediate family group. She was Phyl, the younger sister of my brother Gene's wife, Marie. She was not really a stranger because we had met more than two years earlier. But it had been months since I had last seen her.

Actually, we had experienced a romantic fling after our initial meeting—I was a dashing soldier boy and she was a pretty, saucy student nurse. That had run its course and we had been completely out of touch for a year or more. Gene and Marie were so enamored with the delights of marriage that they had arranged that original meeting for the two of us. They should have known better than that. Everybody knows that "arrangements" just don't work. At least it hadn't so far.

On Thanksgiving Day there on the couch we exchanged few words; our eyes said it all. Hers said, "I love you." Mine said, "I love you too."

But my mind knew better. *There is no way. This is impossible. It's crazy! How could a perfectly beautiful, reasonable girl even entertain such an irrational thought?*

Nevertheless it had happened. A stormy, tempestuous romance had begun—"the 'eyes' have it."

That night, in the quiet solitude of the hospital ward, I savored every moment of the day. The ebullience of the earlier hours had subsided and reason had returned. Realistically, a romantic involvement was the least likely prospect of all.

For starters she was already engaged to a fine young

chap who had recently been discharged from the Navy. He had stormed in from California and overwhelmed her with a sparkling diamond. You just don't break in on a scene like that. She had known him in high school. He was a member of her lifetime church affiliation and lots of other things were in his favor. But most of all he was a healthy, robust specimen in full possession of all his faculties.

By comparison I didn't have a whole lot to offer. I faced undetermined months of hospitalization and reha-bilitation. It had begun to dawn on me that the fleeting hopes of recovery I had secretly nurtured were slowly evaporating. What girl in her right mind would want a half-lifeless man?

In spite of her engagement to the ex-sailor, she began a regular program of visitation—three transfers and two hours by bus each way. An uncommon amount of effort for just a friendly visit. The rationale for these visits was simple. After all, we were shirttail relatives of a sort. It was all in the family.

Bill, to whom she was engaged, was a tolerant type but he couldn't help being curious about the whole business. Why would his fiancée go to that much effort to visit a pseudo brother-in-law? What kind of missionary mind did she have? He was determined to find out.

A visit seemed to be the only way to go, so he boarded the Foster Avenue bus. Since he was a displaced Iowan by way of California, Chicago transit circuits soon left him "short circuited" and he was nearly three hours arriving at the hospital. He must have thought his bride-to-be a little whacko to go through that kind of serpentine journey to see someone who figured so casually into her program.

Presenting himself at the nurses' station he inquired as to the whereabouts of patient Frost. He was directed down the hall to the first door to his right. Quietly entering the four-bed ward he timidly inquired as to which patient was the one he sought to visit.

He was a total stranger to me and his visit was unex-pected. Impulsively I turned to the patient in the next bed,

"Isn't that the young guy they took out on a slab last night?"

Without a moment's hesitation my roommate responded, "Yup."

There was a heavy moment of silence before our visitor backed cautiously from the room and headed back toward the nurse to report her "error." He was hardly out of hearing before we broke out in convulsive bursts of sidesplitting laughter. We had no thought of how unfunny and macabre our feeble effort at humor really had been. The little joke was short-lived. Next thing I knew, an extremely irritated nurse was charging through the door. Her fiery eyes pierced the semidarkness as she pointed her finger straight at me and barked, "*That* is your Mr. Frost."

I mumbled some awkward effort at apology. The visit was necessarily short because his arrival was fairly close to the end of visiting hours. The conversation was strictly surface but at least he had found out what he wanted to know. This sallow-faced paralytic was certainly no threat to his relationship with his girl. That was for sure.

It doesn't pay for a fellow to be all that sure.

Years would pass before I would see Bill again.

The matter of Phyl's visiting me at the hospital had been settled. Of course she could go as often as she wanted. It was obviously a noble effort on her part to make that horrendous trip occasionally. But the visits became more frequent as the grip of winter loosened and spring would have its way.

A part of the cadet nurse program at the northside hospital where Phyl was training was a final six-month internship at one of the major welfare hospitals in the Chicago area. Two would be sent to Hines Veterans Hospital. She and Jeanne, a close girlfriend, began to systematically spread the word that Hines would be the least desirable place to spend that final span of training. They were so successful that when the bids were all in, they were the only two submitting for Hines. Their subtle campaign had worked and they were automatically assigned.

It was six months of soul-searching and intrigue. One of the cardinal rules for the young cadets was absolute—no fraternization with patients. If that was the case what purpose had been served by Phyl's chicanery to get the Hines assignment?

At first her work station was in the far reaches of the establishment. It was simple for her to dress in street clothes after work and present herself as the same visitor who had visited so regularly during the previous months. As shifts changed and her assignments moved closer to my ward, the visits were frequently made in uniform. She didn't dare come directly to the ward so our meetings took on a clandestine nature, spending our time together in the central canteen or at the ends of long hallways near a ready exit.

More than one night the "snoopervising" nurse made the turn into the hallway at a distant intersection. Reluctant to separate, there always seemed to be time for one more lingering kiss. As she perched precariously on the arm of the wheelchair we embraced tightly until the old girl was nearly upon us. At the last moment Phyl would spring from my arms and disappear through the exit into the darkness of the night. I was left to face the wrath of the red-faced "hall patrol." It was amazing how confused I would be on those occasions. I could never recall names other than my own. I seldom seemed to recall the situation of just moments before. At least not with the same clarity as my detractor. The episode usually ended with a harsh warning that it should never happen again. But it always did.

It wasn't like we didn't have a plan. If we had ever been caught flat-footed, or maybe I should more appropriately say red-handed, we would use the old relative dodge. After all if her sister was married to my brother that made us some kind of relatives. Being related should make the fraternization rule null and void. We never did find out whether our well-rehearsed defense would hold water or not. We never had to use it.

I didn't mind the cat-and-mouse games with the supervising nurse corps, but formidable opposition was right around the corner. Back on the home farm in northwest Iowa the news of a budding romance between the youngest daughter and a helpless cripple was devastating. Phyl's father, Nick, had migrated from Holland on a cattle boat at age 17. If a fellow couldn't literally put his shoulder to the plow from sunup to sunset he was automatically disqualified as a potential provider for his precious daughter, the ninth of his ten children.

Nick felt obligated to set the wheels in motion to reverse this very dangerous and unthinkable trend. This meant mobilizing what limited forces he could muster. Marie was the answer. Had not she been the one to introduce us initially? She lived in the Chicago area, so naturally she was elected to wage war against the relationship. She tried, but I'm not sure her heart was in it. Her feeble effort was to invite the two of us to dinner and then whisper quietly in the kitchen to Phyl during dishes. It was probably the most effective way to encourage the continuation of our falling in love. Bless her.

Big brother Gene had only one rejoinder. "Why don't you leave the kids alone!" I'm sure, as a young preacher he was firmly convinced that marriages are established in heaven. "What God hath joined together, let no man put asunder."

Since Gene and Marie were apparent failures, eldest sister Kathryn was summoned to campaign by mail. A virtual blizzard of letters began arriving from Ocheyedan, an old Indian haunt in the upper western corner of Iowa. The letters made distressful reading but did little to assuage the fervor of our passionate love for each other. Actually they served as a vehicle to further cement the bond that was forming between us. I think Phyl also heard from Pierce, Clarence, Elmer, Ray, Don and Leona. Only her younger brother Ervin couldn't cared less. No doubt all of their interests were well-intentioned but fruitless.

In desperation her dad struck on the ultimate weapon.

For the first time a breach was in the making. He offered to fully pay all expenses required for her to achieve a college degree. It would require a separation of several hundred miles and a solemn promise from Phyl that she would completely and forever renounce this "frivolous infatuation." Up to this point we had chuckled happily together over all the futile efforts that only succeeded in bringing us closer together.

But this one wasn't funny. It had the ominous sound of potential success. We were sitting in one of our favorite romantic retreats up on the northwest side of the city. Phyl broached the subject matter-of-factly, "I have a letter from Dad. Let me read it to you." I don't think I even extended her the courtesy of letting her explain her reaction to his proposition. It just sounded like she might go for it. I was furious. The whole cockeyed idea was unthinkable.

"How can he do this to us? What has he got against me? He's just a farmer that never went to high school! What does he know about the twentieth century?" Oh, I was angry and had to express it. Phyl's plaintive efforts in defense of her dear dad fell on deaf ears. I was deathly sick of being reminded that I was totally unacceptable as a potential son-in-law. "Nuts to it all. If the whole family doesn't want me, then let's call it quits. I don't want them either!"

With that I started the engine of my new hand-controlled Oldsmobile with a roar and jammed it into first gear. The rubber howled on the asphalt as I raced toward the major artery back to the city. Phyl screamed with fear, "Watch what you are doing! Are you trying to kill us both?" to no avail. I simply squeezed my hand tighter on the motorcycle-type accelerator and raced headlong through the traffic. Upon reflection, it was one of the most stupid things I had ever done. She was right. We both could have been killed.

Since she had graduated from her nursing school and no longer worked at the veterans hospital, I dropped her off most unceremoniously at her rooming house. Back in the ward the lights were out and most of the patients slept. I sat pouting by my bed. There was no sleep in me. While I wallowed in self-pity I heard my name whispered quietly. It was Joe, one of my roommates.

Joe had been there nearly as long as I. We were getting to be old-timers after 18 months or so. Our friendship had grown into a close relationship. His black hands lay helplessly at his sides. Because of his inability to pick up a fork, I often fed him his meals. I had to admire the guy. He was always smiling. Regardless of his condition, which doubtlessly was permanent, he just kept smiling.

In the dim light of the ward his teeth glistened behind that ever-present smile. "What's the matter?" he inquired. It wasn't the first time he had volunteered to hear my tale of woe. Nor was it the last.

"I'm through with Phyl. I don't think I ever want to see her again," I spouted. Joe was privvy to the ups and downs of our romance. He also intuitively knew that I was talking nonsense.

We whispered together for the next couple of hours. Both of us had placed our faith in God long before, but somehow, Joe, in his seemingly tragic circumstance, was keeping in touch in a way that far surpassed most of us. That night as I clasped his black hand in my white hand I realized afresh that God loved me, that He loved the both of us without respecting one above the other. Just as importantly, Joe succeeded in reassuring me that God has a very special plan for all of us; that He had a singular plan for my life. If that plan included Phyl, then the very gates of hell would not prevail against it.

After all these years I can still see him sitting by his bed with a stylus in his teeth turning the pages of his favorite book. He daily searched the Scriptures.

When it was determined that I should have my tonsils removed, a young intern was assigned the task. I was assured that it would be simple, quick and painless. Well, it was "none of the above." After 45 minutes the whole place was splattered with blood. Particularly the poor un-promising doctor. His superior mercifully returned to find out what was taking so long. "Holy cow!" he cried, "What are you trying to do to this man? You have long ago removed his tonsils and successfully removed a good bit of throat cartilage!" By now I wished I had been given some-thing other than local anesthesia.

Though I had been a patient there for nearly 26 months, the policy was that all tonsil patients be dis-charged within 48 hours of surgery. I was sicker than I had been in nearly two years, but it made no matter. The U.S. government had its regulations. So my stay at the VA hospital ended abruptly.

I drove out of the main entrance with a deep sense of gratitude for the many pleasant memories stored up dur-ing my long stay. After the pain had left and I was able to say no to sleep medication, the months passed swiftly and pleasantly. There were rich memories of educational ther-apy with my therapist, Blossom. She encouraged me to write creatively. Frequent visits with renowned persons such as Paul Harvey were good medicine. The occupa-tional therapist kept me busy for hundreds of hours en-graving copper and sterling silver jewelry.

At times physical therapy was something resembling a medieval torture chamber. If you have never experienced galvanic therapy, hook up a wire from a 110-volt circuit and tape the tip to your gluteus maximus (your hindside, to the unsophisticated) and turn the switch on and off every few seconds. You'll know what I'm talking about. The result is downright breathtaking. Or try this: lie on your back and raise your leg as far as you can. Then allow some unfeeling oaf to pull it another foot or two past that position. Ouch! That can make you wince.

There were more pleasant moments: hundreds of hours in the Hubbard tank with hydrotherapy; equally as many trips struggling through the parallel bars, giving the illusion that I was actually walking.

I shall always remember those patient souls who labored so faithfully and expertly to restore the loss.

The culminating effort was exerted by the vocational rehabilitation counselors. Since I could no longer pole-vault or run the high hurdles, a thorough battery of assessment tests revealed that there was only one thing in life for which I was eminently suitable to pursue. Horology. Yes, I should be a watchmaker. It mattered not that I inwardly aspired to the lofty calling of medicine; that decision was simple—people in wheelchairs did not become doctors. I guess the assumption was that if your legs were paralyzed, your mind must be too.

I pondered the counselor's advice as I turned westward into the late afternoon traffic.

I started in at Watchmaker's College in Elgin, Illinois the following week. It was the perfect rehabilitation program for me. There wasn't a moment to sit at home and generate sympathy for myself. It required my attention from early morning 'til nightfall.

Home for me now was an addition to the house which Gene and I had occupied years earlier before it was finished. Dad had built a special accommodation that included a small bedroom, a living room and an adequate bath. The long sloping ramp was easily transversed in the worst of weather.

Gene and Marie lived there now. He was serving as the pastor of a local church. He wasn't a Sunday-only preacher; he practiced what he preached seven days a week. I was often the special object of that practice. If you don't believe that preachers of the gospel assume the role of humble servants, I wish you could have ridden piggy back with him up to the second floor as often as I did.

"Greater love hath no man than this . . ."

This particular night was Christmas Eve. Dad and Mom were free of their duties at the Boys School, an unusual occurrence at a holiday time. It was an intimate gathering. Dad, Mom, Gene, Marie, Phyl and me. A big surprise was in store for everyone.

My sweetheart's sailor had returned to California

shortly after determining that the hospital patient was no competition romantically. His diamond followed him by mail shortly thereafter; much to his dismay, Phyl had sent it back. Now it was my turn to dress up her finger. It mattered not that I had borrowed the money from her to buy it. The beautiful promising pact was sealed that night beside the Christmas tree. Phyl, the diamond and the night were beautiful. So was life.

I think the big brother and sister rather expected it but Dad and Mom were in a state of semi-shock.

It had never occurred to Dad to have a man-to-man talk with me since that drastic turn of events over three years earlier.

But now he called me aside and quietly questioned my sanity. It was all in Phyl's behalf. He, like Phyl's dad, had also farmed for many years and it was difficult to see how I could lead a normal life with my physical limitations. It wasn't hard to convince him that ours was a permanent commitment. There would be no turning back. It was a Christmas Eve to remember.

The next morning we huddled together in the back of the little church and wept openly as we celebrated the birth of Jesus. Christmas is a glorious time.

The winter passed quickly and uneventfully. As the wedding date drew near, Phyl invited me to visit with her folks out at the old homestead. Nick had determined that he would not be attending the wedding. He simply couldn't give his blessing to the proposed union. We reasoned that a brief visit of a few days might change his mind. I should have known I wasn't very welcome when lunch on the first day was served in the basement. It was grossly obvious to all that I was powerless to join them. Phyl was embarrassed to tears and pled for a consideration of the reversal of the roles. "How would you feel?" she cried. It was to no avail. The two of us ate silently in the kitchen.

Sunday presented an awkward problem of greater proportions. The company of believers where the family worshiped was a pretty closed communion. Visitors were an occasional curiosity but a visitor in a wheelchair would be a singular event of great magnitude. Everyone would have a stiff neck from craning for a better look. In counseling together the family agreed that the kindest choice of all would be to let me "sleep in." A real gesture in favor of *my* comfort and well-being.

There was no alarm and I'm generally a pretty heavy sleeper. That morning was no exception. Everyone managed to get dressed, have breakfast and get off to church without arousing me. Phyl reasoned that since I wouldn't be going to church there wasn't a thing to be gained by both of us staying home. Out of respect to her father she felt obliged to attend with the family.

I awoke with a start. The silence was deafening. It became immediately apparent what had happened. *What a fine kettle of fish this is!* I thought. *I'll show them.* With that I quickly dressed up in my Sunday-go-to-meetin's and developed a plan of action. Heading toward the door I came to the sudden realization that two men had rolled my chair up those steps and there was no way I could get down alone. After checking all doors leading out it looked as though the front porch had the best possibilities. While there were four steps, the total fall didn't appear to be much more than the height of my wheelchair.

That was it! Slide from the chair to the floor of the porch. Drop my chair to the ground. Then carefully slide over the edge of the porch into the chair. From there on it would be a breeze. Whistling enthusiastically I managed the maneuver without mishap. If it hadn't worked to precision I would have spent my Sunday morning in the tall grass of the front yard. Thanks to the many hours of training at the hospital for special situations, the plan was successful. With the chair flipped into the back seat of the hand-controlled Olds I was on my way—to a different church, you may be sure.

The steeple of an old church across town from the family parish caught my eye. Judging from the enthusiastic reception they gave me I reasoned that they must have had few visitors in wheelchairs from out of town in times past, particularly arriving unescorted. A friendly deacon was soon plying me with penetrating questions of every nature. I couldn't resist dropping a clue that if sufficiently prodded I had been known to sing a solo in church once in a while. Moments later he returned with a personal request from the presiding reverend. The special music for the morning was temporarily indisposed and would I favor the congregation with a vocal number.

The response was immediate. "Do you want one or two?"

"Why, uh, two of course." What else could the poor man say after that entrapment. And so two they got. And with the songs they also got a mini-sermon by way of introduction. I was positive word would get around the countryside before too long; I would never tell about it, but *they* were bound to hear. You can imagine my exhilaration when the weekly paper featured an article on the visiting guest soloist from Chicago. I have always been invited to the family church from that day on, whenever I'm in town.

The wedding date was upon us and what a glorious occasion that was! Since Phyl's parents were still opposed and not planning to attend, the entire planning and preparation fell on the two of us. Thanks to a host of local friends, things came together in a wondrous symphony of caring cooperation. The big day arrived. The church was selected because it was at ground level and convenient to the chair. I wasn't about to ambulate down that aisle on a couple of "sticks." I'd been to weddings of friends where the groom had nearly fallen and was caught and propped back on his crutches. Not me. I had even seen normal two-legged guys faint and fall dead away at their weddings. If I had a fainting spell in the chair not too many would know about it.

The church was a little on the expansive side. We assumed that, because the guest list was not too long, the crowd would be on the small side. What a shock to peek through the door and find the place filled to capacity. It seemed like every casual acquaintance in town had come. I don't know what kind of a circus they expected; we were only two ordinary people to be joined in holy matrimony.

The best man was my oldest brother Lyle, my gracious benefactor during my last year in high school. While we were alone in the dressing room leveling our bow ties and fastening our boutonnieres he made a stab at a seven-minute cram course on "The Way of a Man with a Maid." It's not like we hadn't thought of the subject before. In fact, it had had a thorough going over. I think he was more concerned than I. After a few moments he seemed to relax. I breathed easier.

The two groomsmen were a couple of real special people. Paul had been a friend that was almost closer than a brother for the past several years. Of particular importance was his faithfulness during the hospital stay. I believe his name appeared in the guest book more than any other. We had worked together in high school, laughed together and prayed together. As I sat waiting for the prelude I recalled the days we dropped water bags into the beer garden six floors below where we worked. Or jumped through the elevated train windows to grab seats before the others could get through the doors. I suspect we were still on the "most wanted" list at the Chicago Avenue precinct station for bombing police cars with tomatoes. Everyone needs a friend like Paul.

Howie was the other groomsman. I would guess the worst thing he had ever done was to deposit his chewing gum on the bottom of a park bench—then I wouldn't believe it unless I had seen him do it. Our idea of a night on the town had been to "cruise" the Fox River in a canoe and sing Negro spirituals to passersby. It seemed like the three of them were the kind anybody would want to stand up with them, no matter how tough a situation they were facing.

Phyl was attended by her sister "Toots" and two nursing school friends, June and Jeanne; Jeanne was the one who participated in the capture of the veterans hospital internship. The cast was a good one.

Gene and Marie finished singing a couple of duets and he took his position at the altar as the marryin' parson. The procession began. The place was beautiful. Phyl and I had pooled our resources and had the place flowered up like the Garden of Eden, which meant we would be on a strict budget on our honeymoon. The organist began the familiar strains of the traditional wedding march and I turned to watch the processional.

My bride was radiantly beautiful in her filmy gown with its train of exotic French lace. It had been an extravagant purchase for sure. Actually it cost more than we had budgeted for a two-week honeymoon trip. But what did that matter? This was a once-in-a-lifetime affair. We would pledge to be one until "death do us part." Her eyes glistened brightly through the veil. She wore a smile of quiet ecstasy. This was her day. This was our day. We would show the world.

I had a lump in my throat as she started down the aisle—lovingly and firmly supported by Nick. At last we had his blessing.

It was 2:00 A.M. before we reached our honeymoon suite overlooking Lake Michigan. What a delightful night it was. Lyle would have understood that his concern was all in vain.

Though it was our usual custom to attend church on Sunday morning, we slept in and enjoyed the ultimate of room service with breakfast in bed.

The next night we spent in an out-of-the-way motel in eastern Michigan. The proprietor took a very special interest in our welfare. He couldn't stand the thought of our spending our entire married life together with me in a wheelchair. He hauled out a piece of equipment which was "guaranteed" to have miracle-working properties. "Here, wear this to bed tonight. Just stick your legs through this ring. Plug this end in the wall. That's all there is to it. It's sure enough guaranteed to fix them legs in no time flat."

Well, what could I say? There was only one way to get rid of the well-meaning fellow. Yes, I would sleep in that silly contraption if he would just quit extolling its virtues and let us go to bed. I will admit that anything that promised a "cure" was somewhat intriguing. Of course it could be purchased for a price. The price we didn't have. In the morning we placed the thing neatly on the bureau and quietly stole away toward our destination.

Niagara Falls exceeded our expectations. It is obviously one of the most awesome, breathtaking sights in the world. We found it hard to believe when some folks commented, "What is so wonderful about this?"

I could not resist the retort, "So what did you expect? That it should be running backwards?"

The most spectacular view was from the deck of the "Maid of the Mist"—hundreds of tons of water cascading down in a thunderous roar just yards from the tiny vessel, dwarfed by the magnitude of it all.

We were not supposed to even be on the boat. The guard at the top had said the road leading down to the dock was for maintenance vehicles only. Our passage was prohibited. Too dangerous. A little friendly persuasion and I was driving my car down the tortuous, twisting excuse for a road. About halfway down I began to regret the decision but there was no turning back. Once aboard the captain approached and inquired tersely, "How in the world did you get here?"

Viewing the falls either day or night had a hypnotic, spellbinding effect that defies description. We never in our wildest dreams could have thought that ABC-TV would send us back to Niagara on a second honeymoon 25 years later. And it hadn't lost any of its awesomeness. "The heavens declare the glory of God; and the firmament [was showing] his handiwork" (Ps. 19:1). There could be no mistake about it.

But we had to move on. The pilot of the tiny seaplane scratched his head in disbelief when Phyl approached him about a ride over the waters of Lake Champlain. There had never been a guy in a chair looking for a ride, at least not as long as he had been in business. Besides that the craft was floating freely some 30 feet from shore in 16 inches of water. "There is no way I can get you into this plane. I can't dock it and I can't carry you."

"If we can get into the thing, will you give us a ride?"

Convinced that it was an impossibility he shrugged, "Of course."

I cast my shoes and socks on the sand, rolled up my trouser legs and chirped delightedly, "Here we come!" I think my bride of eight days was having second thoughts but she was a trooper. Gripping the handles of the chair we headed straight for that midget-sized amphibian. The poor pilot was dumbfounded. Once convinced that he had a fare he pitched in to help, and the three of us finally made it into the cockpit without falling into the drink.

It was a memorable flight.

We had made no specific plans other than the stop at the big Falls. We drifted leisurely around upper New York, investigating the backwoods roads and drinking in the breathtaking beauty of the Adirondack Mountains. Occasionally we stopped along the road and prepared our meals boy-scout fashion. It's amazing how tasty a breakfast of fried eggs and sausage is when fixed and eaten in the chill of the early morning in a grove of birch trees.

About dusk one night we wound down into a valley and were entranced by a lake that seemed to stretch as far as we could see. The sign by the side of the road was a revelation of the originality of the first settlers in the area—LONG LAKE.

It didn't hurt to let people know that we were on our honeymoon. Nothing was too good for us. Most folks had never met an odd couple like us before. The operator of some cabins at the point of the lake arranged for us to have the best housekeeping place he had. The first two days there it rained steadily. We had laid in a store of groceries and really didn't care how long it rained. We were so much in love. God had brought us together in spite of all that opposition. We simply basked in the warmth of His goodness.

The third morning was clear and dry. Having experienced a touch of cabin fever we were up early looking for adventure. An old native in the boat business agreed to rent us a skiff with a very small motor. I thought of asking for a can of caulking compound; but I could swim pretty good regardless of the useless legs, and there was a life jacket for my wife. I slid into the stern seat and hauled on the starter rope. It kicked right off. Phyl tossed the chair into the bow and clambered aboard. We had been told that there was a resort at the far end of the lake that could be reached only by water. Why not? Let's go there for lunch.

About halfway there the mail boat passed, nearly swamping our tiny craft. We literally gulped in the scenery. Locals fished and sunned, waving folksily as we passed by. Arriving at the resort shortly before noon we were surprised to find we had traveled well over 10 miles since launch. Forget launch, let's lunch. The day was soon spent. We were having such a great time I had forgotten how long the trip up had been.

Friendly but apprehensive hands pushed us adrift. Setting the rudder on a homeward course I twisted the throttle to the full position and we headed back. We had completely forgotten the admonition by the vendor to be sure and get back before dark. The sun falls abruptly behind the mountains. The suddenness of twilight to darkness should have alarmed us but we were thoroughly enjoying ourselves. Not until an inky blackness enveloped the scene did we experience some uneasiness. It was obvious that the light at the far end of the lake was still a couple of hours away and we didn't even have a running light. I idled back the throttle a bit. As slow as our speed was, a submerged log could flip us out of the boat. We sat quietly listening to the muffled purr of the outboard and the quiet slap of the water against the prow.

Several angry men met us at the dock. They had begun a search shortly after sunset but had abandoned their effort because of darkness. They were hoping we had stayed at the lodge for the night. I tried to dispel their anxiety by assuring them that I was in complete control of the situation. It had been simple to get a fix on that tiny light near the end of the dock. The "Light" had led us home.

Our budget for the two-week venture had been a grand total of $180. It was a real lesson in economics but we had fared well. However, it was some 800 miles home and we didn't have the price of another night's lodging. The only solution was to head for Illinois. We pulled into the home driveway around 2:30 A.M. exactly two weeks and nearly 3,000 miles from our departure. There was a hundred-dollar check in the glove compartment that Dad and Mom Hibma had given to us after the wedding, but we were too proud to cash it. Our stubborn independence had had an early start and we aren't easily broken. We had $1.85 left in the purse. It was enough.

That was a fantastically glorious honeymoon. Would that all able folks could have an equally fulfilling, satisfying experience. We had come a long way since that silent eye conversation on the couch Thanksgiving Day, some 30 months earlier.

Thank you, God.

Chapter 5
From California to Capetown

California, here we come!

A series of biopsies had been performed on my lower limbs and feet because my legs had developed draining sores. It was a mysterious malady that apparently baffled a host of medics. Old Doc Jones, who was resisting retirement like the plague, finally fell upon the solution.

"Since you don't have enough sense to come in out of the cold, you had better move to a warmer climate."

Now, why hadn't anybody else hit on that idea? And how right he was. I could figure out more reasons to sit out in subfreezing weather than anybody in town. Once my feet were cold it didn't seem to make much difference when I warmed them up. Watching football on November afternoons in Chicago can be really chilly. I never have gotten that game out of my blood.

California! I had been there once in the summer of '46, sent as the family "medical corpsman" to nurse Grandpa Gooden back to health. With the family patriarch back on his feet I managed to purchase a cheap ride back to Chicago. It was cheap alright. The other paid fares, a couple of young sailors, were as angry as I when the driver told us "so long" in Oklahoma City. It's a long hike from there to Chicago. Flat broke, I bummed my way back home, thumbing rides and sleeping in the grass along the road. There are some who surmise that was the beginning of the end of my physical well-being.

Now Phyl and I would be going together to establish a new life away from our immediate family and friends. We were going to stay with Grandpa and Grandma Gooden. The idea was to go as soon as possible. Get those legs warm. I was tired of those nasty draining sores on my calves and the soles of my feet.

We didn't have much of a bankroll. Moving would be a real adventure in faith. We hastily got our affairs in order and made plans for an early departure. There was no money for a moving van so we bought a one-wheel trailer to move most of our worldly goods. That little trailer was never built to carry the load it was asked to bear. Miraculously, it did.

A day or so before we were to leave a well-meaning neighbor lady engaged Phyl in conversation. When the lady became aware that we were about to begin our pilgrimage unaccompanied she blurted out anxiously, "But surely you're not going to go all the way to California without taking a *man* with you, are you?" It took all the resistance I could muster to refrain from saying something I would forever regret. I just simmered.

Having bade friends and family farewell we began the long trek west. In the dead of winter it would have made sense to head toward the most southerly route. Not us. Due north. Had to see as much of the family as possible on the way. We had no fear of heavy snow and icy roads. Didn't that dear neighbor lady know that we wouldn't really be traveling alone?

So it was up into Wisconsin, Minnesota, northwest Iowa, Nebraska, Kansas, across the panhandle of Oklahoma, the tip of Texas, across those beautiful monotonous wastelands of New Mexico and into Arizona.

I was happy to leave New Mexico. We had stopped for dinner at a small roadside diner. I was pretty used to the idea that people couldn't resist taking a second look whenever we showed up someplace. It was before the days when larger numbers of wheelchair people were taking to the road. It would forever remain a mystery to me why the waitress in that diner, or any other, would make the strange inquiry, "And what would *he* like for dinner?"

No legs, no brains?

The entire trip was a journey through a winter wonderland. The scenery was breathtaking for us flatlanders. The most breathless moments came in the old mining town of Jerome, Arizona. Cliff-dwelling Indians didn't have anything on those folks hanging on the mountainsides of that town! Driving up the street in one direction, we looked straight down several hundred feet to the houses we had just passed going the other direction.

Hand-controlled automobiles were a recent postwar phenomenon. The brakes were activated by a vacuum tank, a system that had been known to fail without warning. I attempted to reassure my white-knuckled wife that everything was under control. If anything happened I could always run the machine into the side of the mountain to save our bacon. Inwardly, I felt composed apprehension. I later admitted profound relief at reaching the relative flatness of the high plateau. The sweet wife relaxed, snuggled close in the crook of my arm. On straightaways I was pretty good at one arm, no feet driving.

Although Disneyland was nonexistent, Phyl thought we were entering Fantasyland as we crossed the Colorado River into California. More amazing than all the sights along the way were those naked, skinny palms, tufted at the top by a sparse green thatch of fronds that seemed to reach desperately toward the azure sky. Certainly the Creator had a good sense of humor. God may have had, but Grandma didn't. Bless her dear heart. The gap between our almost childish newlywed demeanor and her advanced 86 years was almost too much to bridge.

The breaking point came one day when Phyl and I had returned from our respective activities. We had just spent the previous week redecorating the kitchen. A beautiful job, we thought. It represented a sincere labor of love. In order to paint the inside of one of the cupboard doors Phyl had removed a tattered, faded planting guide that had been clipped from a newspaper many years before. It had been thumbtacked to the wood. We surmised that it had not been used for years.

That made little difference to Grandma. While we were at work she redeemed that ancient relic from a storage shelf and replaced it exactly where it belonged, inside that cupboard door! This time she did not use a thumbtack but a three-inch nail. That spirited little arthritic five-footer had mounted a stool and hammered that "priceless" guide back in place. Phyl was wounded to the quick upon entering the kitchen. That nail protruded two inches through the wood. Its ugly point had cracked the new paint and splintered wood two inches in each direction. Without a word she marched to our bedroom and broke into tears.

"I never wanted to come here in the first place. We need a house of our own. No young couple ever moves in with grandparents."

Inwardly I knew she was right. I found myself between a rock and a hard place. Weren't we really doing this for my mother who was concerned about the welfare of her aging parents? Hadn't my grandparents been more than gracious in providing us a place to land after our dislocation from back east? Wouldn't we want someone to look after us when we were their age? My pitiful arguments fell on deaf ears. Honestly, I knew she was right but I was loath to admit it.

There followed the first major spat of our extended honeymoon. We had only been married eight months and this wasn't supposed to happen for years. But it did. In her haste to rush past me and out the door I grabbed her arm and pitched precariously sideways in my chair. The door jamb saved me from going clear over but Phyl was gone and out the door. It took a few moments to right the blasted thing and follow down the ramp after her.

By then she was well down the street hotfooting it to who-knew-where with me in pursuit. I'm glad it was dark. The scene must have resembled something out of a "comi-tragedy." Clickety-click, clickety-click, the little wheels rattled in the cracks of the sidewalk. Phyl was not so far ahead that she couldn't hear the clicking sound. She slowed her pace until I was abreast. Silently we circled back to the house together.

That night there were tender words and gentle reminders of the lifelong commitment we made at the altar before God and all those witnesses. Tomorrow we would look for a home of our own. That night was in some respects sweeter than that first night of the honeymoon.

A home of our own wasn't out of the question. The G.I. bill was paying my way at the local community college and Phyl was also making adequate wages as a nurse for a nearby general practitioner. We have chuckled many times over how she got that job and with whom. Years before, the California ex-sailor to whom she had been engaged had shared plans to make their home in California and Phyl could work for the family doctor. Of course those plans never materialized.

Shortly after we arrived in Long Beach she ran an ad in a large metropolitan paper. She stated simply that a "Christian nurse desires position." Response to the ad was immediate and she was hired. It wasn't long until the cat came out of the bag. This was the very doctor with whom she was tentatively promised employment by her suitor back in Chicago some three years before. An amazing turn of events.

In the meantime I had thrown myself wholeheartedly into a business administration major at school. I soon discovered that the most beneficial approach to the educational process was a balance of the curricular and the extracurricular. The hours I invested in student politics and forensics in particular have served me well over the years. I thought that being student body president would give me enough fiscal clout to get myself sent to the National Oratory finals. It didn't. Winning "State" had to suffice.

Crossing campus one afternoon, another chap in a wheelchair stopped me. "Have you ever played wheelchair basketball? We practice at the armory three nights a week. We could use a guy your size."

"Wheelchair basketball? Never heard of it, let alone play it. You have to be puttin' me on." I have to admit I was pretty skeptical. I had not been the world's most artistic dribbler when I played that senior year in high school; it could be worse in a wheelchair. "I doubt if I have time for it but I'll come down and watch."

I didn't watch for long. This looked like something I could get interested in doing. It looked a little like a combination of football, basketball and general mayhem. I had always liked to mix it up. You can believe I was on hand for the very next practice. Thus began a 15-year association with the sport, the first six with the famous world-renowned Flying Wheels. My wildest dreams could never have devised a scenario equal to my experiences with that game.

By the following year I had developed sufficient skill to be invited to travel with the "Wheels" on a barnstorming tour that would last for nearly three weeks and cover over 12,000 miles. It was a whirlwind tour, visiting cities as far away as Boston and a dozen or so major cities in between. Since the "Wheels" were one of the first such teams to organize in the country, if not the first, we usually gave a pretty good account of ourselves. We were fiercely proud of the fact that our club was made up of genuine "gimps," while many of the opposing players walked to their chairs using canes or crutches. In spite of their physical superiority we couldn't wait to whip their socks off. We did more often than not.

One of the many highlights of that adventure occurred in Washington D.C. Phyl was traveling with us as team nurse. Her presence had been a godsend as flu and "walking" pneumonia had devastated the team. More than one night she got only moments of sleep while tending the needs of our troops.

Every place we stopped seemed to be our oyster. Washington especially. The best accommodations, the finest cuisine and always folks stumbling all over themselves to make our stay more pleasant.

One particular morning a group of Grey Ladies from the American Red Cross was escorting us about town. The Lincoln Memorial, Jefferson Memorial, the Washington Monument and more. This was Phyl's first trip to our national capital so it was particularly exciting for her. Since our group was fairly large we had seen little of each other during the day. One very attractive lady seemed to take a liking to Phyl and the two chattered happily together. She seemed to have insights into the Washington scene beyond normal expectation.

At lunch in the Senate dining room we finally came together, seated opposite each other at the table. It was my first opportunity to directly address the lady. "And where is the senator today?" I inquired.

"Oh, didn't you know? He is so sorry not to be able to join us for lunch, but he has the flu today."

Phyl's eyes revealed her surprise and dismay. All morning she had known this gracious person only as "Pat," just another Grey Lady. Now for the first time she became aware that her charming escort was none other than Mrs. Richard Nixon, wife of the notable senator from California. It was a touching commentary to the commonality of us all. We were later to meet with the senator in his office. Our reception by him was no less gracious.

Months later we met again at a political rally in Long Beach, California. I had been asked to serve as the master of ceremonies. The platform was filled with dignitaries. There was the governor of California, a U.S. senator, the mayor, several congressmen and Nixon, the vice-presidential candidate. He seemed somewhat surprised to see me there. I was nearly dumbfounded when he passed right by the governor and the others to shake my hand and say, "So good to see you again, Wally."

Wally? I had only met him once, nearly a year before, and then as one among a large group! I was impressed, really impressed.

Phyl and I were to meet him one more time. He had invited us to meet with him in the private recesses of Angel Stadium, not because of us but because of our son. By then our son David was a more familiar name to him; he had become a fan of two David Frosts—one the commentator and the other the baseball pitcher.

Oh, yes, back to basketball. There were so many hair-raising episodes on that trip it is difficult to recall them all. One took place in Kansas City. We were traveling in a DC-3, the work horse of air transportation. It was a good thing too. That plane had a way of forgiving human frailty and even stupidity.

We were scheduled to take off promptly at 8:00 A.M. The laborious task of loading all those paras, their chairs and the gear had been completed. Let's go! The only problem—no pilots. I recalled having seen them late the previous evening moving through the lobby at a somewhat less than steady gait.

A full hour had passed when a couple of raunchy-looking characters with bloodshot eyes came rushing up the narrow aisle. "Oh, no," I whispered to Phyl. "Those two drunks aren't going to try and fly this thing today, are they?" Phyl didn't respond. She stared grimly out the window. I asked myself how long they were supposed to wait before flying after imbibing. It didn't seem to me that enough time had passed. And apparently it hadn't.

Those nitwits fired up the engines and taxied to the end of the runway. It was a subzero day in February. Common sense dictated that the mandatory engine warm-up would have to be longer than usual. My heart fluttered slightly as I realized that there would be virtually no warm-up time. Full throttle was applied and the little ship was rolling for takeoff. The roar and vibration made conversation impossible. We gripped hands and smiled reassuringly to each other.

There was a tremendous ear-shattering roar. The craft shuddered violently as the brakes were applied and throttle cut. It came to a halt scant yards from the levee that separated the runway from the now-frozen Missouri River. We were later to learn that a carburetor diaphragm had failed and there had been an explosion in the engine with subsequent loss of power. That should have ended the idiocy for that day, but muddled heads prevailed. We sat in that plane waiting for "repairs" for more than seven hours in numbing cold before a decision was made to go back to the hotel for the night.

Another fright that most of the passengers missed out on was on the final leg of our flight back to Los Angeles. It was somewhere near 4:00 in the morning. My ears were usually sensitive enough to know when there was a change in altitude. I had awakened in response to that sensitivity. I nudged Phyl awake to let her know that we would be landing soon. I wanted to spare her the pain that can come from not chewing gum or yawning when coming down in one of those pre-pressurization cabins.

Peering out the windows I could see that we were in a pretty heavy snowstorm. Although the wing light was barely visible I assured Phyl that we would fly out of the "stuff" before landing. However, from the sound of the engines, it sounded very much like final approach. "Naw, it can't be. They can't land this tub in zero visibility."

But incomprehensibly, they tried. We never did touch the ground. There was a sudden surge of power and a dramatic change in attitude. It was obvious the pilot was trying to get somewhere in a hurry. Up! The explanation given to me later was incredible. We had flown right by the tower less than 50 feet from the ground. The tower operator had seen us. The pilot had seen neither the ground nor the tower.

On both occasions we had been only a heartbeat or two from eternity. A good God spared us one more time.

"Why, God, why?"

"God bless you, Mr. President," I stammered nervously. I knew we would be seeing Mr. Eisenhower in the now familiar Oval Room. It never occurred to me that I would be shaking hands with him and having to carry on even the most limited conversation. If I had had a clue I might have made an effort to prepare a little speech. But, on second thought, I probably would have forgotten that anyway. Under the circumstances I could hardly recall my own name.

The previous evening we had played the Richmond Charioteers from nearby Virginia. It had been a hotly contested fracas before the patients at Walter Reed Hospital. The President had been present. He liked it. It was a "blood and guts" affair that apparently appealed to his military nature.

By that time I was beginning to establish a nefarious reputation as one of the "big bad guys" in wheelchair basketball. At least there hadn't been too many that played quite so rough. It really wasn't that I was so "bad," it just seemed that when I felt a bit too crowded, I simply raised my elbows a little like a chicken. If the opposition was too close it had an upsetting effect on them. Upset usually meant they went sprawling out of their chairs to the floor. This constituted a foul—that is, if the officials were looking. They weren't always looking.

I must admit my deportment in that game was probably not up to presidential standards, but it did spice up the game considerably. And it wasn't all one-sided; I was out of the chair and on the hard wood myself several times during the evening. The President was to remind me the next day that I played the game a little like General Patton might have done. That was high praise.

All I could think to say was "Thank you," and "God bless you, Mr. President."

One of my most cherished mementoes is the autographed picture of the two of us shaking hands. It hangs over my desk for all the world to see.

After that I pledged to refine my game. An All-American team was picked annually at the national tournament. Every participant aspired to that kind of recognition. The "Wheels" had stormed the country on tour that winter and figured to finish high in the nationals. And we did; we took the championship. The team that won was usually well represented on the All-American roster. I figured I had little chance. I still carried the "bad guy" image and besides we had a couple of real hotshots who could shoot the lights out. My job was to rebound and deliver them the ball.

"And now for the All-American team." The M.C. began to intone the representatives from the third team. Five names were called. I was not among them.

I leaned over to Jack, a young Pentecostal preacher. We had roomed together for years on these trips. "Jack, I think that takes care of me. Now we'll have to wait and see whether you and Fritz make it." He and Fritz not only made it but were named first team.

But before they were named, the second team was called out. After four names had been announced I had completely dashed the idea of any recognition. Instead Jack and I were busily contemplating first-team possibilities.

"And missing first team by just one vote, Mr. Wally Frost." I nearly stood up! It may not have been football and the major networks may not have been filming it for the evening news but it was a milestone.

Having been a part of the barnstorming tour for six years, several of us broke away from the "Wheels" and formed a new team in 1957. We won the national championship in our first attempt. That time they won without me.

No one could understand why I declined to play in the championship game. Few understood then and probably less now. The final game had been switched to Sunday. I had 10 boys in an eighth grade Sunday School class back in California. They had believed me when I encouraged them to put their attendance in that class as a number one priority. I couldn't think of a good reason why they should be in class and I should be out playing basketball. Right or wrong, I didn't play. I was again named second team All-American. No play, no first team. I've never regretted that decision.

The most spectacular chapter in the wheelchair athletic history was yet to come. I had been playing for a long time and had seriously contemplated putting it aside. By now I had the responsibilities of a job, five children and the like. I was teaching at Valley Christian High School in Artesia, California.

The phone rang. "This is Tim Nugent calling from the University of Illinois. We are planning a lecture-demonstration tour to Africa. Would you be available for two months to participate? We need to know right away—pre-trip publicity, rosters, resumés—lots of details to be worked out." It's a good thing Tim is a good talker. I was speechless.

"Why, er, uh," I stammered, "I need to check the dates. It starts nearly 10 days before school is out. I'll have to clear it with the principal and the superintendent. They don't get too excited about their teachers taking off that early."

I had heard this trip was on the drawing board. The idea was that only graduates from the U. of I. would be invited, a cross section of wheelchair people who had made good in a variety of pursuits in the workaday world. The world's number one education-rehabilitation center takes great pride in many successes, but mainly in their 100 percent success rate at placing their graduates. The closest I had been to the university was as a deadly combatant against the famous University of Illinois wheelchair basketball team, the Gizz Kids.

They had been so committed to using their own people that it came as a real shock when I got the call. I didn't ask why or how, nor did it take me long to clear the school calendar. The biggest hurdle was at home. It meant that the man of the house while I was gone would be all of nine-and-a-half years old. Dave would be helping Phyl with his four younger brothers and sisters, the youngest having arrived only one month earlier. The good wife readily agreed to a two-month stint at "widowhood."

She would be alone, yet she wouldn't be. Like it said on the plaque on the living room wall, "Christ is the head of this home, the unseen guest at every meal, the silent listener to every conversation."

We didn't even have the price for the fare to Illinois, which was the only cost we were asked to bear. My mother came to the rescue as she did so often. What a saint!

A short orientation and training period in Champaign and we were off to New York. After participating in the national games it was up, up and away to Africa by way of London, Rome, Salisbury and into Johannesburg, South Africa. Loading logistics was a major factor every time we moved, which was often. The attending crew did a marvelous job getting the 17 wheelchair travelers on and off planes and buses, sometimes several times a day.

The reception we received was simply fantastic. The crowds that came to watch our participation in swimming, track, archery, basketball and even football were wildly enthusiastic. This kind of involvement by the disabled was at the very limits of their comprehension and certainly far beyond their practice. Before we left the country, many were thoroughly convinced paraplegics can "adjust," that they can be "entirely self-sufficient and self-supporting." The acclaim was overwhelming. I was thrilled and grateful to be part of it all.

Besides speaking and demonstrating at schools, sports arenas and hospitals, two of us found even more to do. When word got about that one of the foreigners was a preacher and that another was a "bathtub baritone" our busy schedule became even busier. Every available minute was taken up with "preachin' and singin'." One Sunday afternoon we shared the basic tenets of our faith on a sand platform next to the rolling surf of the beautiful Indian Ocean. On a Sunday evening we shared the speaking time in a black native church on the outskirts of Johannesburg. It was a new experience, having our words translated into the Zulu tongue.

Our visit to that church nearly led to an international incident the next night. In our enthusiasm to be cordial and Christian we invited four young students from the church to attend our performance at a major indoor arena. We had completely forgotten that blacks and whites didn't share the same roof under any circumstance. It was not until they mentioned my name as having extended the "special" invitation were they admitted. I found out later that their presence nearly brought the roof down on the lot of us.

Tension in South Africa was apparent to even the most casual observer. One morning I asked our lovely hostess, with whom Jack and I were staying, to stop the car so I could get a picture of a black standing in front of some significant graffiti scrawled on a wall. She panicked briefly and respectfully requested me to put away the camera. I'm not sure how I convinced her to draw up to the curb but just as I brought the camera into view the black subject quickly raised his paper to cover his upper half. Everybody seemed nervous.

Having completely circled South Africa from "Joburg" to Pretoria, Welkom, Bloemfontern, Capetown (that's near 12,000 miles from home), East London, Port Elizabeth, Durban and Pietermaritzburg we headed up toward Central Africa to visit the Rhodesias, since renamed and repoliticized.

If I hadn't known better I might have guessed that Victoria Falls was the original site for the Garden of Eden. More awe-inspiring than Niagara and far more natural. With a couple of days available we left the grandeur of the V.F. Hotel and headed for an overnight stay in Wankie National Park. The white hunter assigned to us proved to be nearly as wild as the animals.

He was committed to showing us more game firsthand than any other visitors had ever seen. Though it was illegal to leave the roads he risked a stiff fine to spend most of the time out in the tall grass looking for lions. Back on the road we found a female elephant with her baby near the edge of a large herd. We were taking pictures like crazy and our guide was determined to give us as close a look as possible. It almost proved closer than any of us wanted to get. We kept backing toward her and then moving away when her ears began to flap. Sufficiently annoyed, she finally charged—four tons of elephant hurtling at us at breakneck speed.

Our "expert" guide shifted into a forward gear again, but this time he engaged the clutch too quickly and that Chevrolet nearly died. We too. Before he had us moving away from that angry beast she had closed to within 15 or 20 feet of our rear. In one of my pictures she is so close that I got only a part of the head in the lens. Great pictures but too close for comfort.

The last stop on that whirlwind tour was grand old London. Our main purpose as a team was to participate in the famed International Games at Stoke-Mandeville in the nearby suburb of Aylesbury. Our forces were strengthened by the arrival of several outstanding basketball players from stateside. Together we took on the world and successfully captured the coveted gold medal. It was a sad day recently when burglars made off with that precious piece of metal I had earned. But it was a good lesson in not laying up treasures in this world "where moth and rust doth corrupt, and where thieves break through and steal" (Matt. 6:19).

After the games we had three days for sight-seeing. "You're on your own. Just don't miss the plane."

Oh, great! No transportation and we had spent practically all our money; also we had no guide. Jack, my longtime basketball traveling partner, and I determined that we would see the sights of that town or bust. So off we went. It was some 35 miles to London Bridge, certainly too far to roll. The American way seemed the only way to go. Up went our thumbs. We made such an uncommon sight that the very first car stopped to inquire about our plight.

"No, we aren't in trouble, we only want a ride to London." The man was too nonplussed to say "no" so he scratched his head and set about loading these two characters that seemed to defy British propriety. He wasn't going far but he did take us to the nearest "underground" station where we could catch a train.

It was perfect. We could roll right into the car. I had never found anything quite so convenient in the States. The English countryside was exotic in its pristine beauty. Nearing metropolitan London, we submerged into the maze of tunnels that form the underground network. There was one slight hitch. No one had told us that the "tube" was several stories below ground when you disembarked downtown. There was no such thing as an elevator. The only way to the surface was by escalator. A longer stretch than I had ever seen before or since. It went up and up and up. Charring Cross station was not made to accommodate wheelchairs.

"No, there is no 'lift' and you are absolutely forbidden to ride the 'stairs' in those machines. You will have to get aboard the next train and disembark at ground level."

Now that we were downtown we weren't about to be deterred. "We'll see about that," I whispered to Jack. "When that security guy turns his back let's ride our chairs on to that escalator, grab the rails and go!" He was game, so in the wink of an eye we made a dash for the moving stairs.

The guard called out after us, "You can't do that!" I wasn't sure what he really meant, as we already were. By the time we reached the top he had called ground level and we were met by two very angry bobbies. They admonished us to never let them catch us doing that again. We didn't. At least not at that station. It was a simple matter of getting off at a different station each time downtown after that.

Since it was Sunday morning a visit to Westminster Abbey for church sounded like a good place to start. We whipped our wheels along Victoria Embankment, around the corner past Big Ben to the famous church only to find the service in progress. Much to our good pleasure they ushered the two of us right down that interminably long aisle right up front.

When it was time for communion, an usher whispered in my ear. Would we like to take part in that aspect of the service? We agreed that we would.

Several hundred parishioners had marched past the altar to receive the elements. After they were all seated we were escorted to the altar, just the two of us. A special ceremony was conducted on our behalf before that multitude. The Church of England had comported itself well that morning. I don't think it was their usual custom to invite lowly Baptists or Pentecostals to the communion table.

The days were filled with exciting adventures from the towering heights of the belfry of Westminster Cathedral to the depths of the basement in Madam Tussaud's Museum. We caught rides on trains, boats and cabs and where we couldn't catch a ride, we rolled. We literally raced from Buckingham Palace, after viewing and photographing the changing of the guard, to Saint James Palace, to Picadilly Circus, to Dickens' house, Old Bailey, Saint Paul's Cathedral, Scotland Yard, Trafalgar Square, London Bridge and the Tower of London.

One of our days was reserved for a visit to Parliament. You can imagine our keen disappointment upon being told that all we could see was Westminster Hall. To get into Parliament required the use of the elevator. The "lifts" could only be used on Saturday. It made little difference to the austere bobbies standing guard that we would be some 8,000 miles away by then. No amount of coaxing could budge their dogged determination. But we were more doggedly determined.

Having circled the building twice without breaching

the guard, we sat disconsolately by the curb pondering our next move. Momentarily a beautiful chauffeur-driven limousine pulled up to the curb and a gentleman alighted. He was impeccably dressed, wore a bowler, carried a valise and an umbrella. He had the air of importance about him.

I grabbed his sleeve. "Hey, Governor, can you help us?" I didn't have a clue to his identity but he looked worth the asking.

He drew himself into a full extension of his stature and stared icily at me. "And how may I be of help to you, pray tell?"

I hurriedly blurted out the frustrations of the last hour. He quietly dismissed us with a brief instruction to report at the main guard gate first thing in the morning. I thought I detected a slight kink in his lip as he strolled toward the building. I think he smiled.

Believe me, we were not a minute late the next morning. When we presented ourselves at the appointed entrance, the guard appeared to be more irritated than when we had made our second appearance the previous day. "I told you that you may not be admitted to this building until Saturday." He *was* firm.

"But yesterday we met a man who works here. He took our names and told us to report here today," I protested vigorously. He stared in disbelief and then asked for our names. "I'm Wally Frost and this is Reverend Jack Chase. We're Americans." I don't think that helped at all and I'm sure he had figured that out already anyway. We waited breathlessly for him to return from an inner office.

When he returned, his demeanor had changed entirely. The icy austerity had turned to a warm receptive manner as he very courteously opened the gate and welcomed us to the Houses of Parliament. As the huge iron gate swung closed behind us he handed us an envelope. Inside there was a simple statement. "Please admit these gentlemen to the Houses of Parliament and accord them all the privileges enjoyed by the members therein." We were dumbfounded. The letter was signed by a distinguished member of the House of Lords, the man we had met briefly on the sidewalk yesterday.

A personal escort was provided for the entire day. We saw every nook and cranny of that historic edifice. The guide showed us things that no "commoner" had ever been allowed to view. It was tourist heaven.

As we were winging our way across the North Pole on the way back to Los Angeles I savored that last day in London over and over in my mind. There seemed to be a very special significance in the fact that "the lord" had opened the door and provided access to the innermost recesses of that place to our everlasting pleasure and joy.

I had met "the Lord" many years before. The British lord was but for a day. *The* Lord was for eternity.

Chapter 6
And Then There Were Five

"And she vowed a vow, and said, O Lord of hosts, if thou wilt indeed look on the affliction of thine handmaid, and remember me, and not forget thine handmaid, but wilt give unto thine handmaid a man child, then I will give him unto the Lord all the days of his life" (1 Sam. 1:11).

Phyl and I had looked eagerly ahead to the days when bouncing, laughing children would be our portion. We both had a deep, abiding appreciation for our brothers and sisters. Her family had numbered 12, mine 10. Our parents had taken seriously the God-given admonition to "Be fruitful and multiply, and replenish the earth" (Gen 1:28). I'm not sure God expected them to make such a generous contribution. On second thought I'm sure He did.

More than two years passed before we began to suspect that a family might not be possible. This led us both to have rigorous examinations by our physician. Neither of us was prepared for the solemn consultation following the tests. "I'm afraid you will never be able to have children. Phyllis appears to be capable but you, Mr. Frost, just don't have what it takes to be a father."

Those words dropped like molten lead on my already disconsolate spirit. Never have children? It was unthinkable. The ride home was heavy with a somber quietness. Somehow we just didn't quite believe him. Past experience had convinced us that even modern medical practice was not infallible. But on the other hand, hadn't we tried every patent remedy that we had ever heard about? Maybe he was right after all and all those people who had tried to discourage Phyl would be saying, "We told you so. We told you so."

We had now been married nearly two-and-a-half years and I was scheduled to head out across country on one of those cross-country barnstorming tours with the Flying Wheels again. My good wife had gone with us once and had felt it to be a tremendous experience, enough so that this time she was content to stay home and continue with her nursing. I think she had some urgent business to attend to, like a prior appointment with God.

It was not as though we had never thought of asking God to bless our house with a child. We had mentioned it often. God always hears and answers when we pray. We were a couple of stubborn malcontents who were refusing to take no for an answer. I believe that Phyl was much more stubborn than I. While I was off galavanting around the country she literally stormed the gates of heaven with a fervency that is hard to describe. She was convinced that Hannah had the secret to fertility—she pleaded for it. So on her knees, in tears before God Phyl asked for a son, fully committed to giving him back to God for all the days of his life.

The answer to her burdened supplication was beyond the proportions of her earnestness. In three-fourths of a year, almost to the day from my homecoming, David was born. And then followed Daniel and Stephen and Rebekah and Deborah, nicely spaced over a 10-year period. God answers prayer in a big way. Bigger than we had ever anticipated. Not only are five children considered to be a fairly good-sized family in this generation but our sons and daughters stand six-eight, six-six, six-four and five-ten and five-nine respectively. Big prayer. Big answers.

When the doctor discovered Phyl was pregnant that first time he was reluctant to believe it. "This is a miracle! It's impossible. I should write this up for a medical journal!" Yes, we knew it was a miracle. Our God is a God of miracles. And Phyl has not forgotten her promise. Even yet, daily she commits not only our firstborn to the Lord but each of the others with equal fervency. At a very early age each child was taken to the altar for a public declaration of that commitment in a joyous ceremony of thanksgiving and dedication.

"Lord, this is your child. We thank you for giving us custody for the duration of his natural life. We ask that you will grant us the wisdom to bring him up in the 'nurture and admonition of the Lord.' We pray that this child will reflect the beauty of Jesus in all he does. We here now dedicate him to that end. In Jesus' name we pray. Amen." That was only the beginning.

When my brothers and sisters were young our dad made a decision to give up his chosen profession as a civil engineer to become a farmer. That way he could be home full time and carry out his role as father. Recognizing the impact of his decision on my life I have declined a number of opportunities over the years that might have interfered with parental responsibilities. I had determined early that being a good parent was just as important as being a good provider. My days would be equally divided between these responsibilities and sleep. With this ratio as a lifelong practice I have slept well.

As parents we certainly have made our share of mistakes. No doubt David was victimized by the first-child syndrome. I don't know how many times I punched Phyl in the ribs in the quiet of the night and sent her groggily to his room to make sure he was breathing. He was nearly pampered to death by a couple of zealots who were oversolicitous, overprotective and downright smothering with our first, very special gift from God. In spite of us, he survived.

We were pretty heavy on the natural things. God did

supply baby's milk in its most natural form so Phyl was more than happy to stick with the basics. After that it was raw milk, raw eggs and lots of raw vegetables. To this day our boys still like their meat fairly raw. As a result Dave was about as energetic a tyke as you could find. Climbing, leaping and running pell-mell he managed to collect some 25 stitches about his face and head before he was six.

You might have thought he had learned by then. Nope. When he was 17 he was still leaping, that time from a 10-foot fence at a local baseball park. He landed smack on his face and was carted off to a local emergency room. No breaks. Just a slight concussion and severe contusions. I will never forget the frustration his high school basketball coach and his parents experienced another time when he took a tumble. In the heat of the championship race he leaped to the wet platform of a trailer that happened to be there for that purpose. In so doing one foot went one way and he the other. You guessed it. A fractured wrist on his shooting hand. He still managed to lead Millikan High to the championship with the help of his long-suffering coach and some very capable teammates.

We would have happily settled for a few stitches, bruises, fractures or contusions. Steve was a different story. At the tender age of six weeks it became brutally apparent that something was radically wrong with the little fella. When a diagnosis was finally determined, emergency surgery was the verdict. "Your baby has *pyloric stenosis*. In order to save him we will have to operate at once."

"Operate? On that little baby? You can't operate on anybody that small." I was convinced there must be another, a better way. The nurse in the family understood that we should sign the papers immediately and let the doctors proceed. The surgeon cautioned that our baby was rapidly becoming dehydrated and we had scant hours to spare.

Pastor Harold had rushed to the hospital to bring comfort and strength in our hour of deep distress. He prayed. He had a way of talking to God that was so direct and so very comfortable. Phyl and I were left alone in the waiting room with a quiet assurance that it was all in His hands. God had provided the physician with special skills. He would give him a steady hand from scalpel to suture.

"The surgery was successful. Your baby will be just fine." We were so relieved, grateful and thankful. Since the surgery had been conducted in the middle of the night we were happy to head for home and rest.

Visiting hours were scheduled the next day at 2:00 P.M. Phyl bolted from her bed early the next morning. Intuitively she *knew* she should go early.

Approaching his crib bed cautiously, Phyl was horrified at what she saw. The little face was blue from lack of oxygen and his tiny body was convulsing violently. A muted scream escaped her lips and she rushed to the nursing station.

"What are you doing for our baby?" she asked. "He needs immediate attention! Where is the house doctor? Hurry! Please do something."

"Your baby is fine. We are doing everything we can for him. Your doctor will be back later to check on him." The response seemed so cold and callous considering the circumstances. Phyl virtually dragged the nurse to his bed.

"Oh, I believe you're right. The doctor should see him. I'll call the house doctor immediately. She will take a look at him."

And take a look she did. And that's about all. With a shrug of her shoulders she admitted that there wasn't much she could do. "Well, I guess I could give him a little oxygen, but you had better call the baby's physician. He should come over and take a look." Then she disappeared in response to the page box on the wall. The whole scene was turning into a nightmare.

A nurse's aide, attempting to comfort the distraught mother, patted Phyl on the shoulder. "I hope you have some good pictures of him. It makes for such a sweet memory."

Phyl ignored the comment as she raced to the nearest

phone. "Doctor, this is Mrs. Frost. Our baby is terribly sick! Please come right away. There is no one here to help."

"Call the house doctor. That is what they are there for," he answered curtly.

"But I did. She has already looked at the baby. She doesn't know what to do. She said I should call you. Oh, please come. Hurry!"

There was a calculating pause at the other end. He never said so but he must have figured that if the doctor in charge did not call him direct, Phyl must be crying "wolf." Rather patronizingly he finally spoke. "Mrs. Frost, it's too bad you are a nurse. I believe you are overly concerned about a normal postoperative condition. The average parent would sit quietly and wait until my office hours are over. I . . ."

Phyl interrupted him almost hysterically. "You don't understand. My baby needs your attention now. He may die before your office hours are over."

Phyl could not believe his parting comment. "I'm sorry, but I have an obligation to this office full of patients. I will get there as soon as I can." With that, he hung up.

She ran back to the room to relay the deteriorating course of events. We were both in a near state of shock. Again we turned to the only source of assistance available to us. It wasn't a very eloquent prayer. It was almost embarrassingly demanding. "God, you've got to do something!"

It doesn't pay to keep your head bowed too long when you really need an answer. We looked up and could hardly believe our eyes—a doctor, a personal friend no less—was striding happily down the corridor. As an orthopedic specialist he seldom, if ever, had occasion to be in pediatrics. This was more than a coincidence.

Phyl frantically grabbed him by the arm. "Dr. Wally, please look at our baby. He needs immediate attention!" And he got it. The good doctor, bless his heart, moved into action. Rushing to the phone he called the baby's doctor. He was able to convey the urgency of the situation where

Phyl had failed. It was only moments before the surgeon arrived on the scene. Throwing orders around like a commanding general, the surgeon took charge. There was a virtual blur of white dashing every direction. Bottles, needles, solutions, chemical formulas and a profusion of medical talk that even the nurse-mother had a hard time following.

The doctor did not leave the baby's side until the crisis had passed. To his credit, he offered Phyl a humble apology. "I'm sorry," he said, "your baby *was* critically ill."

We have been eternally grateful for that miraculous happenstance. Had it been any other day at any other hour we would have lost our little Steve.

Dan was probably fraught with more mishaps than the lot of them put together. We were visiting relatives when he was a mere toddler. Exploring the recesses, closets and stairs of a new environment he managed to push open a basement door. Stepping through into the darkness he tumbled over the side of the unguarded stair and plunged ten feet to the concrete below. Landing on his head may have saved him. It was weeks before the grapefruit-sized swelling disappeared from the side of his head.

He must have been about five when he tried to "swallow" a curtain rod. Well, not really; it just looked that way. With the sharp raw end of the rod in his mouth he attempted to get to his feet. The result was a vicious laceration to the roof of his mouth. He nearly strangled on his own blood and vividly recalls the suturing without benefit of anesthesia.

A year or two later he was astride his new bicycle, too accomplished to need training wheels. He was ready for street riding. Since we lived in a residential neighborhood the streets were relatively safe. Or so we thought. Just as Dan left the drive to enter the street, a notoriously reckless driver from the other end of the block roared around the corner and sent bike and boy flying. Contrary to our initial expectation the damage was relatively minor. One mangled bike that could easily be replaced; one fractured collarbone that required pinning together by surgical procedure.

He also managed to give us quite a fright when he was a junior in high school. When he persistently complained of abdominal pains the doctor was called. Since flu was in season the doctor treated him accordingly. He prescribed pain pills to alleviate the discomfort. The pain passed and Dan resumed his activities.

The next night the pain was back and more severe than before. It was 2:00 A.M. You always hate to call the doctor in the middle of the night, especially when you know he seldom has a night of uninterrupted sleep. The temptation was strong to give him another pain pill and wait until morning. Again medical intuition dictated otherwise. Phyl called the doctor and said she was bringing Dan to the hospital. It took some coaxing to convince him that it might really be that serious, but he grudgingly agreed.

Bundling Dan into the back seat of our old station wagon, we headed for the hospital. An older brother, who shall remain unnamed to protect his reputation, had used the car on a date the night before and had arrived home on some of the last fumes in the tank. The old clunker gave out about a mile from the hospital.

It was an unlikely scene. Me with a wheelchair, Dan, desperately ill, huddled in the back seat. And Phyl afoot on a dark street looking for gas at 3:00 in the morning. Providentially she found a one-legged fellow in a nearby all-night laundromat. He volunteered to drive her to the nearest all-night station for gas. I guess you might say we arrived at the hospital by "trial and error."

Fortunately, the doctor's arrival coincided with ours. He immediately flew into action. The diagnosis was burst appendix with severe complication of peritonitis. There was no time to lose. Again skilled hands, God's guidance and emergency prayer saw us through another crisis.

Although it was touch and go for a couple of days, Dan survived to play another day. He had been relatively small for his age up until then. But after that appendix was gone he just grew and grew and grew.

There are those who say boys are easier to raise than girls. It hasn't been so at our house. Come to think of it though, Debbie did manage to fall out of a tree and break her foot when she was small. Becky, who was seldom underfoot around the house, got underfoot of her horse, Sapphire. It was only a small break. No cast required. Aside from that they haven't suffered much more than a headache or an occasional bout with the flu.

It certainly helps to know that the lives of our children—that all of our lives are in God's hands, in His place, in His time.

I recently read in the paper that a judge had ruled a father unfit to raise his two boys solely because he was a quadraplegic. The good judge should have lived at our house for the past 32 years. It would have been fun showing him how unlimiting it is to raise a family of five while in a wheelchair. (The decision was reversed later and the quadraplegic got his boys.)

The action never seemed to stop. The common denominator of doing things together was the basis of every activity. The first thing we did after Dave was born was to attend the First Baptist Church of Lakewood together as a family unit of three. As our family grew over the years Phyl and I were committed to never send them to church but to go with them. Children need to know that "man shall not live by bread alone" (Matt. 4:4). As parents we can have confidence that having trained "up a child in the way he should go," we can rest in the peaceful assurance that "when he is old, he will not depart from it" (Prov. 22:6). That is not to say that he may not nearly starve to death spiritually while trying to live on "bread" alone. Nor does it necessarily mean that our children will not at times walk "in the counsel of the ungodly." It simply gives us the confidence that God will fulfill His promise that "all thy children shall be taught of the Lord; and great shall be the peace of thy children" (Isa. 54:13).

We were always of the opinion that the children should have firsthand knowledge of our rural roots. This meant taking several trips from California back to Illinois, Minnesota and Iowa over the years. My, what pilgrimages they were! Most of the trips were in station wagons. When the children were small the back was roomy enough for them to string out like a row of sausages to sleep. The ever-present wheelchair reserved the space directly behind my driver's seat. Our baggage made up a very lumpy bed for the kids.

These were usually low-budget trips. Mom made sandwiches of bologna and cheese as we drove and passed out lemonade for dry, parched throats. A stop for hamburgers and coke was a very special treat—usually a reward for a few miles of peace among the restless natives. Motel rooms for a growing family were costly so I usually tried to drive long days and sleep short nights. This meant checking motel after motel around the midnight hour to try and find the "economy size." My dear wife was a tremendous help. She was glad to have me drive. I was even more pleased to have her in charge of the children, finding the right motels and doing the bulk of the loading and unloading. We were a team, yet we were one. We worked it all out together.

In Iowa there were cousins everywhere. Most of Phyl's nine brothers and sisters lived in close proximity. Her oldest brother was not to be outdone by her dad, so he had ten wonderful children of his own. To visit all those aunts and uncles and cousins was a real "down on the farm" experience.

One very special night we were visiting their cousin John in Minnesota. It had to be one of the clearest nights of that or any other summer. In southern California you can count the stars, but on a very dark night on the plains they are numberless. It was about midnight, long after the boys' usual bedtime, but I was determined to find them some falling stars. Not just a few either. We went out to the blacktop and the three of them sprawled out across the road on their backs, transfixed by the awe-inspiring beauty of that canopy of stars. It wasn't but a moment until a delightful squeal punctured the silence. "There's one!" and then, "There's another!" How long we stayed I don't know. I think the boys could have stayed all night. They saw more falling stars that night than they had seen in a lifetime up until then.

Our last big trip together was in the summer of David's fifteenth year. It would be the last time he would have time for an all-family outing like that again. We had purchased a big black used Lincoln—the most deceiving thing I had ever done. Everybody, I mean everybody, thought I had come into some big bucks. In reality it cost me less than a new Chevy. I could drive that thing almost anywhere without being challenged.

The logistics of that trip were different than any we had taken before; it was the first one in anything other than the old faithful station wagons. By now David was six-feet-four. By the time we got the chair, the gear and all seven of us in that car there wasn't a square inch to spare. David's favorite spot was right behind me. That way he could extend his legs up over the front seat with a foot extending past my head on each side. That must have created a bizarre appearance to passing traffic.

Since it would be our last trip together we decided to make it more of a sight-seeing trip than usual. That was a blessing in disguise. We would never have survived if it had not been for those frequent stops that permitted everyone (except the driver) to unwind, stretch and relax momentarily. I usually drove off a bit to take care of the natural processes with whatever makeshift arrangement I could find. Then it was apply the shoe horn, reload and force close the door! It wasn't all peace and harmony either.

Living together in those cramped quarters day after day frequently led to friction and dissension. We used every trick in the book. We sang, we recited, we read, we played word games. We made up games, we destroyed games, we laughed and we cried. Their mother became a specialist at diversion. To this day if there is tension brewing in the house someone will say, "Oh, isn't that a lovely cornfield out there?" That usually results in a good laugh and tranquility prevails.

My defenses were less subtle. Having wearied of trying to drive with one hand and reach back to whack the appropriate protagonist, I hit upon a simple solution. Just turn up the radio a little at a time. Before anyone was aware, the rear speakers were blaring so loud that no one could hear the other. At that point fussing was futile. When the rearview mirror told me that the strife had ceased, the radio slowly returned to normal.

That summer we saw more, did more and had more fun than ever before. Dave and Dan recall catching their first big walleyes in northern Minnesota. Dave remembers even better the "eye" he got from Grandpa Hibma. Grandpa was about to boat a big one. It looked to be the biggest hookup of the day. Dave grabbed the net and, in his anxiety to boat it, proceeded to knock Grandpa's big one right off the hook. We all learned a little about patience from Grandpa that day.

Dan recalls a big "eye" he got from Dad. Dan was always so handy with everything and usually proved to be a big help to me in nearly every situation. That day Dave, Dan, Steve and I were fishing from a country bridge. The bullheads were biting and Dan was eager for me to get in on the action. He not only got me a pole but proceeded to cast for me. Thoughtful lad. One problem. The keys to the car were in his hand as he cast. The lead weight landed far out in the lake. So did the keys. Dan always dared to risk.

The boys didn't do all the fishing. Mom and the girls took a fling at baiting a hook a time or two. While Grandpa supplied fancy lures for the boys on the big lakes up north, the girls had to be satisfied with little Iowa Lake using grubs or night crawlers. Yuk! Getting those slimy things on a hook was a caution. But their efforts didn't go unrewarded. A six-inch perch brought squeals of delight. Of the thousands of pictures taken on those outings, none tells a story better than the fishin' shots.

To share the details of our family adventure that year would result in a special travelogue edition. Over all those years of travel, thousands upon thousands of miles, we never experienced anything close to a major problem. We never traveled alone. God was our unseen passenger.

———————————

I have vivid recollections of an open-door policy at our house. Dad and Mom welcomed everyone except the gypsies who tried to steal the chickens. I was particularly impressed with the presence of five smiling black faces seated with us at the dinner table, a traveling singing group from Tuskegee Institute. Most of the locals had seldom, if ever, seen black folks, let alone have them for dinner guests in their own house.

I never saw my mother turn a hungry stranger away from our door. I think my folks were careful "to entertain strangers," being aware that "thereby some have entertained angels unawares" (Heb. 13:2). Phyl's and my home would be that kind of home.

Shortly before our first child arrived, a young marine visited us with a friend. It became evident that he had limited family ties to which he could cling, and they were thousands of miles away at that. He scratched his shaved head in disbelief when Phyl handed him a key to the house. He was given permission to go and come as he pleased, whether we were home or not. Before he left for a term of duty in Korea he handed us the pink slip to a brand new car. No amount of protestation could deter him. It was ours. He wanted to give it. We owned it. That settled it. A powerful lesson concerning bread cast upon the waters. Through the years our doors have been open to individuals, groups, and weary travelers.

For many years Phyl was hostess for the neighborhood Good News Club. Recently we received a letter that best depicts the long-term value of just one of many activities. The letter was from Texas. More than 20 years earlier the writer had given her heart to Jesus at one of those club meetings. Though she had wandered for years in the shadow of that decision, she finally had "come home" like the prodigal son. She now has a lovely family of her own and is the hostess for the Good News Club in her own neighborhood. "Mrs. Frost, I just want to thank you."

Jesus, we just want to thank you.

The memories from those distant years of my childhood have served as a potent guiding force. Lessons learned early are not soon forgotten. During the depression Dad was poor as the proverbial church mouse. Often in church he would stop the collection plate and make change before he passed it on. He never failed to give sacrificially. He was still doing it until the day God called him home.

We have often failed God in that regard. But when we have had the courage to step out by faith the results usually exceeded our wildest expectation. I was serving as a deacon at First Baptist Church, Lakewood, California. A building program required a very substantial sum be raised. We reasoned that if all the doctor, lawyer and banker types gave enough, the rest of us could get by easily. After all, we had three little boys by then and my private-school teaching salary was not exactly excessive. But something within our spirits said simply, "Trust God." Together we prayerfully decided on a figure far beyond our current ability to pay. God would have to supply.

The due date was drawing near and we had not saved a dime toward the total we had pledged; neither had God supplied. So we determined to raise the money through a bank loan. The banker listened to our proposal to pay over an extended period of time. He finally asked for what purpose the money was to be used. When we said we were going to give it away he blanched incredulously. The loan offer was withdrawn directly.

We were back to square one. A few days later I noticed huge, billowing clouds of black smoke rising from the general direction of home. The closer I got to our house the more apparent it became that the fire was a considerable distance from our street. No danger. A huge oil refinery fire was in progress a couple of miles away. It burned for many hours, totally destroying the refinery. It was a newsworthy event.

Upon arising the next day we discovered that an oil rain had fallen on the entire neighborhood. Every house would have to be washed and painted. The oil company's insurance adjustor was soon knocking on our door. Would we settle for the estimated cost of a professional wash and paint job? "Reluctantly," we agreed. The two of us promptly geared up for a big job. Phyl on the ladder and me on the ground with a paint roller fixed to an eight-foot handle. No professional painters could have done a better job. The insurance settlement was within a few dollars of our commitment to the building fund. We know God doesn't burn down refineries to help folks meet financial obligations. But as long as the thing was burning up anyway, why not a faith-building byproduct?

As parents we have made our share of mistakes and then some. However, we have always tried to give parenting our best shot. A little extra love can cover a multitude of error. The bumper sticker asking if you have hugged your kids today carries a depth of truth beyond the practice of many parents. Seated in a chair kept me more the children's size when they were little. That allowed for lots of little games. Wheelies, powerhouse, chair climbing and, yes, even boxing. All of these provided ample opportunity for physical contact. The kind of flesh-pressing that leaves the youngster feeling wanted, accepted and loved.

I probably retire to my bedroom more frequently than the average dad in order to take a little pressure off my rump. Consequently much family time has been spent frolicking on our king-size bed: wrestling, punch-outs, pillow fights, TV time, reading, hair combing and story telling.

In later years I've spent many hours massaging sore,

athletically abused muscles. There is nothing like a dad seriously kneading the aching legs of a 21-year-old in the middle of the night. It's obviously more productive than huggin' the big hulks.

How often have I heard parents exclaim vigorously, "There will be no pets around our house. I can't stand the mess." I will have to admit that there have been times when we were less than enthused about the creatures: when a cat had kittens where she shouldn't have; or a puppy proved it couldn't be fully trusted in the living room. Be that as it may, a child whose spirit has been crushed for whatever reason needs to cuddle and converse with a family pet. The therapeutic value of that experience cannot be measured.

It's amazing how natural many of the lessons of life can appear to a child—propagation, birth, life and death. There has been more than one funeral, accompanied by real tears, grief and a final committal back to the earth in our backyard.

Phyl has patiently survived turtles, pigeons, rabbits, hamsters, cats and dogs. To this day the entire family insists a collie be kept at the home place. She gets as warm a greeting when members of the family come home as anyone else present.

It's amazing how children thrive on praise. If we as parents have a regret, it is the wasted, damaging words of criticism we said in anger. Some of those moments were not without redeeming value. Many is the time we have had to swallow our pride, admit our error, say, "I'm sorry" and ask for a child's forgiveness.

But we weren't always wrong. Sometimes those little rascals could get into the most unprintable mischief. Both of us have always been firm believers in the proverb, "Correct thy son, and he shall give thee rest" (Prov. 29:17), modern psychology notwithstanding. Phyl shared equally in the disciplinary function. There was never any of this "wait until your father gets home." Children respond to correction so differently. One of our children has never had any more severe discipline than a stern look. The eyes always got results. While another has been on the receiving end of more whacks than were probably deserved.

It has always been a mystery to the children's peers. They frequently asked, "What do you do when your dad is mad at ya? Don't you just run away? He can't get you then."

I can't explain exactly why, but that has never been a problem. The boys in particular have always given a singular answer, "If my dad is mad at ya, you *don't* run!" I guess you might say we developed a mutual respect for each other early.

Our house has never been too heavy on rules. David, the firstborn, probably felt the heavy hand of regulation more than the rest; Debbie, the last, the least. It has never been terribly important to be in bed at a specific hour. Slumber parties sprang into being spontaneously. We always had confidence that we could trust our children to hold their own in "learning" situations. How else could they learn to stand on their own two feet? There were two very rigid rules: they always had to let us know (1) where they were and (2) when they planned to be home.

To the best of our knowledge the children have never had a concern about their dad being "different." As far as we can tell, I wasn't. I recollect only one occasion when one of the younger ones was a little unsure about my first appearance at PTA. There always has been a sense of "family." Each member of the group was fiercely zealous for the others. As far as I know, no one made the offer that "my dad can beat up on your dad." At least I hope not!

I suppose much of the family feeling stems from the many things we did together, many of which we couldn't afford. But somehow, afford them we did. There may not be a whole lot in the family estate when we are gone but memories will be rich.

One of our first investments was a volleyball court in the backyard. It was good sized—24 by 48. It also served as a track for tiny motorized racing cars, tetherball, and basketball off the back of the garage. That old hoop still hangs from the roof. I call it our $25,000 basket as it has paid for two major college scholarships. The volleyball court has paid for itself several times over, but not as handsomely as basketball. It all added up to hours and hours of family play.

Later we put in a pool. Doctor's orders. Good therapy for me. The kids were getting big enough to clean my clock at most any kind of game; no more games of one-on-one in basketball, or placing a volleyball out of their reach. But in the water it was different. I could pretty well hold my own.

The backyard was the center of family activity for years. Not just for our family but for much of the neighborhood and even the community. I sometimes thought we had lost our minds when the church busses emptied eighty "Chappy Chipmunks" off for a swim.

You can only keep 'em in the backyard so long. We have always been thankful for "community." First on our priority list has been the local church with its Sunday programs, the camps and clubs. These activities have been broadly augmented by the YMCA, Campfire Girls and all the leagues from "Little" to "Connie Mack." Busy children tend to make good children.

It hasn't been all play either. They have always responded readily to the traditional American work ethic. Their jobs have crossed a broad spectrum from careerist at a downtown department store to selling peanuts at the beach.

Dave always got a job that paid by check. Steve often carried his home in his socks. Dan got his first "big job" by answering the question on experience—no frills: "Huckster."

Many have asked how we managed it. Especially from the wheelchair. I think there is simply only one answer. *We didn't do it alone.*

Chapter 7
Too Soon to Quit

More than one person had inadvertently expressed the soulful sentiment, "Uh, it's too bad, uh . . ." or "It's such a shame, uh, well, you know what I mean." After all, if a dad is stuck in a wheelchair, what help can he be in active sports? Why not stick with chess?

While chess is a challenging game, it lacks the kind of punch I need. Punch? Hey, now there was an idea with merit. So before Dave was old enough to throw a ball accurately we obtained a set of hand-me-down boxing gloves from the cousins. Dave's first introduction to sports was by way of the "manly art of self-defense." He never seemed to get used to my stiff left jabs on his nose. Baseball sounded like a viable alternative. Anything would be better than boxing! I guess he was all of six, but big for his age.

The backyard was still undeveloped at that stage. It had not yet been torn up for a pool. So the yard provided an 80-foot distance which became our "ball park" until we were ready for Little League. Dave was a fast learner. He soon concluded that it was better to catch that mean round thing than to let it sting his shins. It wasn't long until we could have a good game of catch that we both enjoyed. The neighbors were awed at the little tyke's propensity to deftly field a grounder and quickly fire it back with reasonable accuracy. More than one was heard to say, "I'll betcha he's gonna be a good one someday." I can just imagine how many will lay claim to that prediction today.

Once you've learned how, playing catch can get old in a big hurry. New game-like conditions needed to be devised. The baseball coach at the high school generously donated a broken bat. So broken that it came in two distinct pieces. No matter. We sawed it off at the end of the break near the "meat" end, salvaged the nub from the handle end, then glued the two pieces together. Result? A neat little fungo-bat of some 18 inches that I could easily handle from the chair with one hand.

Now we could play for real. Sharp line drives, wicked hopping ground balls and pop flies that came nearly straight down—these had to be caught or else. "Or else" sometimes turned out to be a pretty sore shinbone or a bloody nose. We never let little things like that deter our progress. Since his brother, Dan, was only four going on five, we really couldn't "recruit" him yet. The rules finally boiled down to this: we would play until one of us was tired enough to quit. Then, starting from that point, Dave was required to field 10 balls cleanly in a row. If he messed up on the first or the tenth, the count started over.

It mattered not that dinner was ready. Or that darkness was setting quickly. Or that there was a chill in the air that contributed to numbing fingers and a stinging palm. Rules were rules. The game was never over until "the last man was out." Occasionally, but not often, compassion overruled. A slight easing of the swing sometimes assured an easy out. More than once before reaching that point his little voice would plead respectfully, "Please, Dad, can't we quit?"

I had read someplace that "it is always too soon to quit." So we never quit. We finished.

Fielding ground balls or shagging fly balls from my chair left a little bit to be desired. Trying to teach him to hit was another matter. We solved it with a rubber-covered drug store baseball and a length of nylon clothesline. Drilling through the ball, we fastened it securely to the line. My end was the handle from a broken jump rope unit. The thing must have measured 10 feet in length. Now we had a perfect pitching machine. I swung it over my head, around and around and around. By the hour we took batting practice: all kinds of speeds—inside, outside, going up or down—more variation than any pitcher could dream up. It was all in the way the rope was swung.

The perfect "rip" would send the ball arching in the opposite direction around my head. That meant change sides and bat from the other side of the plate. It worked like a charm until a foul tip off the end of the bat would send the ball whistling right past my ear. "Hey, knock that off! If you'll just keep your eye on the ball you'll hit it solid every time."

He did learn to hit that thing pretty solid too. Probably the most memorable hit I can recall was in Dodger Stadium. Dave ripped a long line drive to right center field off a fair-to-middlin' pitcher, Don Sutton. It was an exhibition game. The American League team pitchers had to hit. A triple? Too bad, all that good hitting potential going to waste in the American League.

Our approach to pitching practice was the toughest task of all. We had an imaginary strike zone that extended about halfway down between my knees and ankles. It was OK as long as he threw strikes. Even balls left or right could be flagged down with alacrity. "Keep it low. Keep it down! They'll hit you out of the park if you come up." Twenty years later I'm still yelling for him to keep it low.

With that kind of encouragement it ofttimes arrived too low and required a quicker reaction than I could produce. The result? A nasty lump on my shin or ankle. We couldn't find any used catcher's gear so again it was time to innovate. A piece of plywood placed in front of my legs did the trick. "Remember, keep it low, Son."

He still keeps it low.

A family friend recalls a Sunday afternoon picnic in the

park. Dave was older then and had established himself on a "Major" Little League team. It's not a picnic without potato salad, ants, a bat and a ball. By then Dan was big enough to take the field as well. The barbeque and the salad had been abandoned early in favor of a diamond. The long flies were directed in such a fashion so as to tax the boys' skills to the limit. Lack of hustle or a misplayed ball was accompanied by solemn critique. The boys were learning early that it takes an all-out effort to win. The friend was later heard muttering to his wife, "They don't play that game for fun. They play for keeps!"

The first real taste of success came on a warm Friday afternoon at the local park. Dave was pitching in the "Minors." It was the typical little league arrangement. The kids with a bit more potential alternated between the mound and shortstop. While most parents sat in the stands, we would drive the old station wagon up along the left field line. When David hit his second successive home run that day I could not resist tooting the horn, banging my hand on the side of the car and yelling wildly, "That's my boy! That's my boy!" I'm sure there was more than one parent that day wondering to himself who that nut was. They probably figured they had at last come across the guy they had heard about all of their lives—you know, that guy who is always "way out in left field."

To this day Phyl, my beautiful wife, the children's mother, insists she calmly sought to quiet my rantings. If I remember correctly she was pounding her fist on the other side of the car yelling, "That's my boy! That's my boy!" After those two homers I began to regret my promise of a hamburger at Bob's Big Boy for every four bases. This kind of production could bankrupt me!

Baseball was never Dave's best game. As soon as the glove went up on the hook after the season ended, the big round ball came off the shelf. By then he was developing more endurance than I could cope with. After hours of "horse" and one-on-one it was I who plaintively appealed for a respite from the challenge. I was more than happy when Dan was big enough to enter the game and give old Dad a rest.

By his sophomore year in high school it was evident that Dave was what both the baseball and basketball coaches call "a talent." A surefire winner. Basketball would pay his way through college. Who needed baseball? It was a slow game. A high school coach has a tough time keeping everyone active at once. Lots of time to sit and get bored. After all, he had been starring in baseball for more than six years. It's called "burnout." One day he came home and announced matter of factly, "I quit."

"Hold the phone! Just a minute now. We better talk this over a little." And talk we did. He had tried football. The doctor had advised that he retire from that game the previous fall. Too much risk of compounding a minor injury. We much appreciated the doctor's candid advice.

That gave me an angle. I reasoned simply. "What if something should happen in basketball? Maybe baseball will have to pay your way through college." Dave allowed as how I had made a good case for sticking it out, so he did. He couldn't possibly ever have dreamed that the very next year would find him on the mound in Dodger Stadium, the winning pitcher in the CIF (California Interscholastic Federation) championship game. Since California is such a populous state it is divided into sections. This would be the equivalent of a state championship in most other areas of the country. What a thrill for Dave! What a thrill for the family! Dad would have loved to have raced to the mound to embrace the big guy. Instead I sat "chair-locked" in the stands.

Oh, thank you, God. You've been so good to me.

Basketball was still number one. Who could have predicted the outcome of his senior year? Another CIF championship? In another sport? Improbable! No, impossible!! Hundreds of high schools had never won a CIF championship in anything, let alone in two sports—and in successive years. It's hard to remember that no kid does it all on his own. Good programs, good coaches and good teamwork—those ingredients make winners. It took me a long time to get used to the idea that Dave didn't win those championships all by himself. Proud dads are impossible!

It's hard not to drop a name here and there when sharing the details. The semis and the finals were held in the Los Angeles Sports Arena. Dave, his coach Howie Lyon, and his able teammates handily disposed of a team from Santa Barbara in the semifinal game. A couple of fellows named Ford and Wilkes were teammates on that club. They later teamed up as members of the Los Angeles Lakers.

The final game was a disaster for the opponents. Out of kindness we'll not name them. It had to be one of the most lopsided scores in all of CIF basketball history. But nothing could dampen the enthusiasm of the thousands of Millikan High "Ram" fans who were there to taste the sweetness of victory. It was raucous. The most ebullient moment of the entire playoffs was reserved for one last final announcement. "And now, ladies and gentlemen—named as Most Valuable Player of the Southern California Interscholastic Federation playoffs, David Frost of Long Beach Millikan High School!"

It was an incredible moment. Simply incredible! By George, I almost got up and walked!

I think Dave would be embarrassed to see a recitation of the awards imposed upon him that year. Just as important as the "Ram of the Year" award was the gold tassle that dangled from the side of his mortarboard.

"Well, Dad, it looks like you were wrong. Basketball *is* going to pay my way through college." He was gracious about it. "But I'm still glad you talked me into keeping on with baseball. Who knows when it may come in handy?"

Scorning over a hundred scholarship offers he opted for a year at Long Beach City College. As a summer diversion he pitched his Connie Mack team to a national championship in Farmington, New Mexico. In order to do that, he had to turn down a trip awarded as winner of "The Dating Game" on national television. I think he felt his

All-Tourney selection was a sufficient award to have made the "sacrifice."

When the baseball awards were passed out at City College that year, Dave didn't even qualify as "a promising prospect." Nevertheless, he still concedes that he learned more baseball from Coach Joe Hicks than anybody else in baseball. Joe taught him the palm ball. It's still one of his best pitches.

Basketball was a different story. Long Beach City College ran roughshod over all comers to win the State Junior College Championship. It's pretty hard for a kid to keep his perspective when winning seemed to follow him around like a shadow. It was always "All-something-or-other." It was probably more difficult for the family to maintain perspective. We are still working at it.

By now Dave was convinced that maybe Dad was right after all. It might still be too soon to give up on baseball. So, much to Coach Lute Olson's dismay and chagrin, his key basketball player decided to transfer to a major school that would permit him to play both sports without reservation. Stanford made Dave a simple offer. "You can play both sports or you can play either one at your own discretion."

Although his decision to attend Stanford had our blessing, his mother and I earnestly hoped that he would go to Wheaton or Biola. Those schools are not what you would call powerhouses but they are "powerhouses" in a more real sense of the word. He was 19. The choice was his.

Coach Olson has probably long forgotten how the veins bulged on his neck when I casually mentioned that Dave had made up his mind and would be leaving after one year at City. He was certainly a prophet in one respect. "Dave, you've always been a winner. You're going to have a tough time getting used to losing." Basketball and baseball wins did come less frequently the next three years. But a sheepskin from Stanford University could hardly be written off as a total loss.

His Stanford days were not without some exciting moments. Stanford was never expected to beat UCLA in basketball. Nor did they in those years. One night in particular we braced typhoon-like rains and raced the clock to arrive in Maples Pavilion on time. It's a long hitch from Long Beach to Palo Alto. The only place left to sit was next to the renegade Stanford band.

From the opening toss it looked like a complete rout was in the making. UCLA roared out to a 10-0 lead. Stanford's Coach Dalmar hastily called time-out. Whatever he said sparked the Cardinals momentarily. Stanford's big, muscular forward, demonstrating exceptional mobility, put some unbelievable moves on an old nemesis, UCLA's Keith Wilkes. When not driving for a lay-up he calmly swished a couple from 22 feet. Time-out. Now Coach Wooden, the old Wizard of Westwood, wanted to talk it over with his boys.

Dick Enberg, one of the more articulate announcers of all time, was calling the game for television back to Los Angeles. With his usual "OH, MY!" he vividly passed on the excitement of the contest to the listeners. He was really passing on our excitement when he actually announced the score as, "UCLA-14, David Frost-10." After all, from a parent's point of view, the Stanford team *was* David Frost. Now that one of his teammates has played several years in the National Basketball Association our scope has broadened considerably.

The end of the line for basketball came during Stanford's annual pilgrimage to Los Angeles for the two-game set with USC and UCLA. Dave had twisted a knee earlier in the week. Considerable fluid had been drained off just prior to the USC match.

USC won that bitterly contested game by a narrow margin of two points on a disputed call that everybody in the house thought was being called in favor of Stanford—at least everybody but the two guys that counted: the "jailbirds" in the striped shirts. To everyone's dismay the call went to USC, providing the margin of victory. The boy had given it everything he had, scored 17 points. No compensation for the loss.

Saturday night at Pauley Pavilion things digressed from bad to worse. The knee was not drained before the game. It was like playing with a cast on his leg. The promised duel with Wilkes never materialized. Keith ran circles around him. The gimpy leg literally glued Dave to the floor. It was the first time in his life he had ever been "skunked" in a basketball game. It would be the last.

A preliminary examination the following week brought a common medical decision. Surgery. They would have to operate. Dave made a better decision. "Let's wait." So he turned in his basketball uniform and went out for baseball earlier than usual that year. The knee healed naturally and has never been a problem since.

It is a rare athlete that does not have a physical problem from time to time. Dave is no exception. A nagging back hindered his performance on the basketball court throughout his Stanford career. The baseball season always brought relief. Although he had not lived up to the stratospheric expectations that Stanford had hoped for, he was an exceptional performer and always gave it his best. Coach Dalmar paid him high tribute when announcing Dave's retirement. He concluded that it was a shame that the world would never know just how good a basketball player David could have been if his career had not been cut short by those nagging miseries. I think I knew.

Stanford was in the thick of the Pac-8 (Pacific Coast Conference) baseball race that year. The scouts had a better chance to evaluate Dave's potential. They liked what they saw. Several talked about a high draft with considerable enthusiasm.

Dozens of scouts were on hand for Dave's final scheduled outing of the season. His arm did not feel just right warming up. Better scratch the start. When the battery was finally announced, a strange hush fell over the stadium. In five minutes the stands were void of scouts. That little twinge dropped him from a high draft choice to the eighteenth round. The Chicago White Sox would take the plunge.

A very embarrassing moment occurred while Dave and I were discussing a possible contract with the White Sox scout in a coffee shop in Palo Alto. Anxious to show off my familiarity with the club I proceeded to tell him about my many visits to Comisky Park "way back when. Luke Appling, Wally Moses and others. Oh, yes, I remembered those guys well." I was carrying on about Luke's unique ability to foul off pitch after pitch until he got the one he wanted. And Moses had the most open stance I had ever seen in baseball. The gentleman was patient—and he was a gentleman. After I had pretty well exposed my ignorance he quietly said, "If you had been looking closely you would have seen me out there at second base." What a "skull"! We laughed heartily.

Dave liked the Sox. Contract negotiations would not be difficult. They weren't. The signing price was within dollars of some who had been drafted as high as the second round.

The signing was a pleasant experience. The Sox representative insisted on coming to our home and explaining the contract in detail. To them it was important that parents know what was going on. No tricks, no hidden clauses, no bad faith. Their candid approach was greatly appreciated. Gary Johnson, the local agent, represented the club's interests and David's interests with dignity.

A privileged few go straight to the big time. The great majority pay their dues through the long arduous journey from "rookie league" to major league. And each year many hundreds never quite make it even after the struggle. It's a sad sight to see grown men who have spent years in the minors go behind a distant bush and cry just after being given their unconditional release. It's the end of the road. No tomorrow.

Dave was not one of the privileged few to go right to the top. The path was a tortuous one—starting in Sarasota, Florida, winding its way slowly north and west. I'm sure he would like to erase some of the memories of those sleazy motels where the air conditioning seldom functioned and the sheets had to be shaken regularly to dislodge tiny lizards or bugs that populated the bedding.

At six-foot-six, sitting for fifteen hours in a bus seat is downright impossible. A thin air mattress strung out on the floor could give some momentary relief. Once Dave thought he had the mattress-in-the-aisle routine beat. Some of the guys found refuge in the luggage racks overhead, but no one quite his size. Sleep came readily. What a relief! Upon awakening, however, he discovered that his big frame had settled in to the point where he could not move. They nearly had to extricate him with the "jaws of life" device. It was probably his first and only bout with claustrophobia.

Being in uniform facing the opposition was also arduous. With the humidity matching the temperature—both over 90—the conditions simulated pitching in the shower. It was not uncommon for Dave to lose 10 to 12 pounds while going nine innings in that unbearably oppressive atmosphere.

As if a fella didn't absorb enough punishment during the regular season with the Minors, management subtly "encouraged" a stint in winter league—someplace like Maracaibo, Venezuela—strange people, strange sights, strange sounds, strange language, strange food. A game could be as dangerous as being caught in no-man's-land between two rival gangs. *"Maten al Arbitro! Maten al Arbitro!"* (Kill the umpire! Kill the umpire!) The only problem was that their wrath was not always directed at the arbiters. More than one ball player had his skull cracked by a well-directed bottle. The best place to go when a riot broke out was into the clubhouse and bar the door.

Yes, the road to the Majors had been long and tedious—Long Beach, Grand Junction, Palo Alto, Anchorage, Sarasota, Knoxville, Des Moines. But to Dave it was worth it now. The wind was blowing off the stockyards that September of 1977 on Chicago's southside when he crawled out of the taxi. But to him the heavily tainted air smelled like French perfume.

"Welcome to Comisky Park. Glad to have you with the White Sox." Roland Hemond, general manager, extended a warm handshake—one of the real class people in professional baseball.

September doesn't allow for a whole lot of exposure for a rookie. Most men would give their best glove for a win, a loss and a no-decision. At least Dave was finally pitching in the Majors.

He had just finished breakfast on the morning of December 5. The phone rang. "Congratulations! You are now an Angel." It sounded too jocular to be for real. His friends were notorious jokers.

"Naw, you're puttin' me on. No way. Who is this?"

The voice on the line was finally able to convince him that he was serious. Dave had been traded to the Angels for Bobby Bonds. He went on to explain particulars of the exchange—Dave Frost, Chris Knapp and Brian Downing for Thad Bosley, Dick Dotson, and Bobby Bonds.

Dave was ecstatic. The Angels were happy. His parents were incredulous. The talk-show hosts were back on their heels most of the time. The fans were venomous, vituperative and vicious. Angels' General Manager Buzzie Bavasi was thought by some to be the biggest boob in baseball. Most suggested that the White Sox had "skinned" the Angels in a "shill" game. One caller even went as far as to say that Dave wasn't worth Bobby Bonds' toenails. I don't think that guy has called in since. At any rate, David was an Angel. A deal is a deal. Mr. Bavasi had the last laugh.

Dave an Angel? Why, his mother had been telling everybody that since he was a little boy. Now she could prove it. Seriously, the whole family was delighted. One of the great thrills of our lifetime.

Still, it wasn't until mid-season 1978 that Dave got his first real shot at a starting rotation. Eleven starts, 5-4, and the team's lowest ERA, 2.59. It's possible the Angels could have used that good arm all year, at least that's what his dad thought while Dave languished on the Angels' Triple A Club at Salt Lake waiting for baseball's digestive system to work.

The recent train of events is fairly fresh in everybody's mind: the dramatic finish of the '79 season to win the West; the disastrous loss to Baltimore in the play-offs; the 1980 season with injuries by the carload. Of all the vocations in this world, few are fraught with more foibles, vagaries and uncertainties than baseball. It's enough to make any man think ahead.

The room is silent except for the heavy breathing of the men. It's a clubhouse meeting. A very special kind of meeting. Attendance is not required but more than half the club has come. The man conducting the session is an ex-ball player. He has discovered that a baseball career is over so very soon. And then what? He doesn't only talk about life but also about eternity. The key question of the day is not, "What will you do with the rest of your life?" but, "Where will you spend eternity?"

David sits near the back. His head bowed, his hands folded. He knows it's the most important question he has ever answered

Chapter 8
Frosting on the Cake

Up to now you're probably thinking, David and Dad grabbed all the headlines in this family. Not so! His brothers and sisters provided their share of excitement around the Frost household. Eventually Dave had to live with a time-sharing system that had some equity. Dave did not grab all the headlines.

Headlines? It was always amusing to pick up the morning paper and discover some new imaginative way a writer would use the kid's family name. "Frost . . . Cool Head with a Hot Hand"; "Frost Chills Opposition"; "Frost, a Cool Customer"; "Frost Puts Freeze on A's"; "Vikings Hoist Frost Warning"; "Frost Proves He Can Take the Heat." After one particularly big win one wag seemed to sum up Dad and Mom's feelings about our little tribe, exclaiming simply, "Frosting on the Cake." There were more. Most brought a chuckle from the reader.

One headline I would like to have written myself concerned our second son, Dan. It would have found its place in the Vancouver, British Columbia papers. "David Slays Goliath!" Now that isn't exactly original, having appeared in the "Philistine Morning Press" some three thousand years earlier. But it certainly would have been appropriate for this occasion concerning—this time—Dan.

The vaunted Russian National Team had been scheduled to play AIA (Athletics in Action)—Canada, the athletic ministry of Campus Crusade for Christ. That in itself was a highly improbable occurrence. The Russians made their bookings months in advance and were not given to last minute scheduling with relative "unknowns." However, Coach Rle (Ar-Lee) Nichols, with a little help from his "chief ally," God, was able to pull it off. Most locals thought he had lost his sanity.

On the night of the game the usual introductions were made with flag and gift exchanges in true international protocol. Most fans assumed that would be the only even match of the evening. The Russians were awesome, towering several inches above their AIA counterparts. As the names were announced by pairs, Dan stepped forward to make the exchange with the Bolshevik Vladimir Tkachenko. As parents Phyl and I really weren't prepared for that encounter. Dan is a good-sized boy, standing six-feet-eight if he tippytoes just a trace. But watching him shake hands with that gargantuan basketball player was too much. There he stood, all seven-feet-five of his massive frame, glowering down at Dan as if to say, "You little runt. How dare you challenge us? We are the mighty Russians. We beat everybody."

And that is what everybody assumed that night. The Russians would massacre the Christians; shades of the Roman Coliseum! AIA got off to a big lead. At least they scored the first basket. I thought that would be their biggest lead of the night. I took a picture of the scoreboard to show the world later that at one point in the game we were actually ahead.

"Oh, ye of little faith!"

The final score revealed how little our faith really was. Dan and the big Russian had dueled all night. Once Tkachenko got his hands on the ball there was no stopping him. The strategy was to keep the ball away from him. AIA managed to do that well enough as Harry, Jeff, "The Ringer" and Scott showed what they could do offensively.

What they did was truly "offensive" to the visitors. Bewilderment and shock registered on their faces at the sound of the final buzzer. AIA-79, Russians-71.

The final score was really not the big issue. The major victory had been at halftime. For those who are not familiar with the specific purpose of Athletes in Action, sports is merely the vehicle for reaching thousands around the world with the good news of the gospel. That night three of the athletes had shared their testimony with the big crowd between halves. Dan had been one to share. Multiplied dozens responded to the simple invitation given there.

Dan had gone through much of the same early "coaching" regimen I had put Dave through, but for some reason he simply didn't grow as quickly as Dave. Consequently he took a lot of guff from many who knew both of them. "Think you'll ever be as good as your brother?" "Too bad you didn't get as big as Dave." And the sharpest barb of all, because it was the truest, "Must be tough to have to follow in your big brother's footsteps."

Occasionally an encouraging word could be heard. Mr. Seymour, Dan's junior high basketball coach, was presenting awards to his championship team. The trophies were all gone and Dan hadn't received one. However, the coach was an insightful man who understood boys. That night he gave Dan an antidote for all of those hurtful barbs. "I don't have any trophies left but I want to make a prediction. There is one boy on this team that will go farther than any of the rest. Dan . . ." (Now everyone knew that the other Dan who had been named Most Valuable Player for the season would be the most likely one.) " . . . Frost is my prediction." It's amazing how kids have a way of living up to predictions.

Although Dan started on championship teams from the ninth grade through his senior year, when the recruiters came around while he was still in high school there was only one major college knocking on his door. At least it was a recruiting trip so he leaped at the chance. When a part of the recruiting trip turned out to be a drive through the infamous "Mustang Ranch," a so-called world-famous "brothel," Dan decided that sticking around home was a whole lot safer than going to that school.

Dan could never figure out why he didn't grow like Dave—he had drunk as much raw milk, eaten as many raw eggs and taken as many vitamins as Dave had. Neither could his parents figure it out. I wanted to salve his feelings a bit so I offered him a hundred dollars if he hadn't reached six-foot-three by the time he got out of high school. I guess he wasn't interested in the money—he graduated at six-feet-four and was six-feet-six by September.

I wouldn't dare tell this anecdote, but Iowa University Coach Lute Olson enjoys telling it about himself. In 1972 Lute Olson was the basketball coach at Long Beach City College. I reasoned that if a major university had shown some interest in Dan certainly the local community would show some interest. But the phone never rang. Not even a postcard. As an involved father I was concerned. I picked up the phone, "Mr. Olson, this is Dan Frost's dad. How does Dan fit into your plans next year?"

"He doesn't. I've lined up all the boys I need. Dan is not one of them." That answer was far more direct and crisp than I had expected.

Not being one to retreat easily I suggested, "Let's have lunch together. At least we can talk about it." And talk about it we did. That friendly conversation launched Dan into an exciting career in basketball. That career is still in motion with AIA. Coach Olson has often told what a "great recruiter" he has been at times.

Not only did Dan start for him that year at Long Beach but he was his number one recruit when Olson moved to the University of Iowa. Their first year together did not result in winning the Big Ten but did start Iowa back on the road to basketball respectability. There were a lot of recognitions for Dan on the way: Most Valuable Player award at the University of Iowa in 1975, Co-MVP of the state of Iowa in '76. Probably the highest tribute of all was paid by Coach Olson when he passed out the pocket-size schedules for the 1976 season. On the back was Dan's picture—"All-American Candidate." Dan has always been glad he turned down, after his two years at City College, 80 or more offers from other schools to attend Iowa.

Did Dan ever take a whack at baseball? Of course he did. He went the usual route of most red-blooded, two-legged American boys. We'll always remember the day he ran headlong into the center field fence at the pony league park; knocked himself plumb unconscious. He held the ball long enough to register an out, but the official was so flabbergasted he ruled it a home run. Dan was keenly disappointed upon waking up in the ambulance to discover that his heroic effort had been in vain. Dan took a fling at pitching too. He once threw a 7-0 shutout in Police League during his senior year in high school.

The coaches at Iowa reasoned that since his brother was such a good pitcher Dan must have the same potential. They saw a long, angular boy with good motion and they could make a pitcher out of that type. Well, Dan got his chance. It was the biggest attendance at a Junior Varsity game in Iowa history. They really came out of the woodwork to see that one.

Dan took the mound. The first one went over the catcher's head. The next one bounced in the dirt. "That's OK. You'll be all right when you get loose." I don't think the batter knew what jeopardy he was in as he stepped to the plate. He was lucky. He walked without getting hit. Matter of fact, the next four batters walked. Dan threw only two strikes in his first 22 deliveries.

As the coach approached the mound Dan pleaded, "Take me out. This is terrible!"

"No, Dan, you'll be all right. Just relax. They'll start dropping in for you," the coach encouraged.

"No! No! I've had it. If you don't take me out, I'll take myself out!" And with that he walked off the mound. His baseball career was abruptly concluded. Iowa won that game 17-2. Dan enjoys telling folks that when he left the game he had a no-hitter going.

You've heard about parents who are avid fans of their kids; I think we were a bit inclined to overdo it. Since I was two or three years overdue for a sabbatical leave, a grandiose idea began to formulate in our minds. The world's leading rehabilitation-education center was at the University of Illinois. Why not study there during the '75-'76 school year? The idea got an affirmative vote from everyone. Now it would be easy to see all of the Iowa's Hawkeye home games as well as most of the away games in the Big Ten. Studying at the University of Illinois was a gratifying experience. Big Ten basketball was so much "frosting on the cake."

The boys have occasionally winced at their dad's exuberance when extolling the virtues of the officials' expertise—or, perhaps more often, their lack of same. Dan was attending an Iowa game the following year. Before the game he was reminiscing with a Big Ten official about some of the games in which he had played and the man had officiated the past two years.

"I want to congratulate you, Dan. You were always a real gentleman. No matter how questionable the call, you always kept your cool."

"Why, thank you, Sir. I always left the marginal calls up to the fans," Dan responded coyly.

"Speaking of fans, I worked a game here last year. There was this heavyweight type down in the corner, right on the edge of the court. He gave me the worst time I've ever had from a fan. I hated it when the ball was on that end of the court. Had a voice like a foghorn. Come to think of it, he was in a wheelchair."

Dan stifled the temptation to answer, "Why, Sir, I believe that man was my dad."

A few people were impressed with Dan's "Hawkeye" basketball career. The Milwaukee Bucks were sufficiently disposed to draft him in the fourth round. That happened to be the year of the American Basketball Association's demise. A hundred and fifty professional ball players were suddenly dumped on the market. Unfortunately that left a lot of first-rate college prospects with nothing more than tryout contracts in their hands. In retrospect that may have been more fortunate than not.

The following year Dan led the Iowa City-based Airliner Club to the National AAU (American Athletic Union) championship. This earned him a well-deserved All-American. I'm sure even Mr. Seymour, the junior high prognosticator, never dreamed that basketball would carry Dan to faraway places like Alaska, Argentina, Africa, Canada and Europe—one junket taking him deep behind the Iron Curtain.

"Dan, you've had an opportunity to try out with two professional basketball teams, the Milwaukee Bucks and the Cleveland Cavaliers. Do you have any regrets at not having played for either of those clubs?"

"No, I honestly don't think I have. I really believe that the affairs of men are out of our hands. I believe I am exactly where God wants me to be."

"Dan, you have no idea how thankful your dad and your mom are that you are right where you are."

Steve has never brought a headline home. No matter. Whereas the shelves are loaded with trophies earned by the other members of the family, he is a living trophy. His closest brush with athletic fame was from the end of the bench during the CIF (basketball) finals in his senior year. I'm not sure they would have won even if he had played. It was somewhat of a miracle that he was even in uniform. Several years earlier he had fallen and cracked his knee on a sprinkler head. By the time Steve was in his junior year the doctor determined that a large piece of bone would have to be removed. Further consultation brought a similar diagnosis but a different solution.

"Removing the affected bone will set up a lifelong arthritic condition. Why don't we try to save the bone?" A nationally-known orthopedic surgeon was speaking. His proposal called for nailing the bone back together—five nails in a circle, into the femur just behind the knee cap.

We agreed. He still has the bone but for all intents and purposes that was the end of any hopes for an athletic career. There is one trophy of his that stands as tall as any of the rest. He still managed to coax enough out of that leg to earn his team's Most Valuable Player award in city league. That is of little consequence. He is first, MVP if you please, in the hearts of his family.

Lest anyone get the idea that he is a no-talent when it comes to sports, occasionally he gets into a game of "horse" with his brothers in the backyard behind the garage. He can really show the big brothers the bottom of the net. He always could shoot the lights out.

Steve doesn't play golf often but when he does I wonder why he doesn't take it up on a regular basis. Be assured, even though he may only play once in six months there are no wagers when his brothers invite him to come along. I like to drive around in the cart and keep score. Recently it took Steve the first nine to get loose. After that he started to roll, roaring through the last seven holes in par. The rest of us nearly swooned when he rammed home an 80-foot putt on the eighteenth! No talent? This boy has some very special talents.

You normally don't associate keeping your girls out of trouble via athletics. It may not be the answer but it sure can help. In an effort to have a well-balanced approach to child rearing we endeavored to balance the "life stool" on four solid legs: spiritual, physical, social and educational. Consequently the girls got their share of encouragement to develop themselves physically right along with the boys. Girls who spend considerable energy at games afield tend to be less readily drawn into questionable social "games" as early as others.

Believe me, our girls would play games! They got the same early instruction as the boys in softball, swimming, volleyball and basketball. Watching our girls play in bobby sox ball is altogether as fulfilling as rooting our boys on to victory. Becky excelled at volleyball in high school—All-League, that sort of thing. Played basketball too. The kids didn't get all the instruction from their dad, either. They still encourage their mom to show off her famous "Iowa hookshot." She can really swish it. And from way out.

It's hard not to mention all the folks by name who generously sacrificed their time to work with our kids. But one needs mentioning. Bent and twisted by arthritis, Joe Romo gave and gave. He was the girls' first basketball coach. He's now had his joints replaced with plastic— knees, wrists, hips—I don't know what all. He is still giving. From a mercenary viewpoint the scholarship money Becky has received for playing college volleyball has paid for the cost of that backyard concrete slab several times over. Unfortunately we will still owe the bank a few bucks when she picks up her diploma at Stanford University this year.

Debbie's energies took a slightly different bent—flag girl at good old Millikan High. Offhand I can't think of anybody in the house who was more dedicated to his or her chosen "sport." If it hadn't been for her many girl-friends who picked her up day after day for 7:00 A.M. practice her mother and I would have had our sanity tested. Now that Debbie is finishing her freshman year at Southern California College she too has moved into the real sports arena. She's excited about her second year of volleyball. The coach thinks she may be good.

Reading about family athletic exploits might give the casual observer the idea that this is all our kids ever did. As parents we get just as much satisfaction out of the girls preparing and serving a special holiday dinner. Interestingly enough, no one can cook and put on a gourmet spread quite like Dan. And when Steve sits down at the piano and plays his own inimitable rendition of "The Sting" or "Come to the Water," we're moved.

A frustrating afternoon during Dave's early years probably sums up the diversity of family activity best. He would rush from Released Time at school to his after-school job, to playing his French horn for orchestra practice at church, back home for dinner and off to night league basketball. Not only did the lad meet himself coming and going but so did his mother and dad. It takes a heap of doin' to raise a family in this generation.

Chapter 9
In Word and Song

I had been diligently practicing the strains of the "Lost Chord" for weeks. The plan was to audition for the Morris B. Sach's Amateur Hour. It was a weekly favorite with a large listening audience throughout the Midwest.

I had never fancied myself as much of a vocalist, at least not in a solo capacity. Oh, I used to sing in the College Church choir but it was very embarrassing when I had to sing the tenor part alone. And the male trio I sang with for the church midweek meeting on Wednesday night was tolerable. It probably wasn't as good as the trio of two girls and me that whipped out a lively number over KROC in Rochester, Minnesota. We were all of 11 or 12 years old at the time.

At any rate, I'd had too much encouragement along the way. Now I was invited to represent Hines Hospital in the competition for a spot on the amateur hour. The audition didn't go badly. I didn't feel much more pressure than while singing in the shower. Surprisingly enough, I was selected to be on the show. I think if I had expected that turn of events I would have managed to be in Timbuktu that weekend.

A few days before the broadcast I unfortunately came down with a bad cold. Three days before the event I had a severe case of laryngitis. I couldn't squeeze off a note. I prayed for a miracle. There wasn't one to be found. Canceling was out of the question. The director was convinced it was a case of "cold feet" so the show would go on as scheduled.

It was awful. Absolutely awful. I don't know when I have been more scared in all my life. I consumed honey and lemon by the cupful. I had a cotton mouth and sweaty palms and the only reason my knees didn't knock was because my legs were paralyzed. The only plus was the fact that this amateur hour didn't "gong" you off the air as they did on the infamous Major Bowes Amateur Hour. On second thought, it might have been better if they had.

The director gave me the signal to take my place before the mike in front of the studio audience. I was on. The results were marginally short of disastrous. Somehow I thinly squeaked my way through the song. The composer must have had me in mind when he wrote it. His "Chord"? Yes, I nearly "lost" it.

At the end of the show Morris himself always announced the placements. I was stunned to learn that I had been awarded first place. Of course there were extenuating circumstances. You see, the judges had been deadlocked on a choice, so the only solution? Award all 10 contestants first place!

It was to be the start of a long career of speaking, singing and MC'ing all around the country from New York to California.

One cold, blustery morning in New York City I slipped out of the Park Sheraton Hotel to roll over to the nearest church. Sitting in the back of this well-known Baptist church on Manhattan Island I recognized a fellow Californian sitting on the platform. Unfortunately he recognized me as well. I was not concerned at seeing him passing notes back and forth with the minister, but I was consternated to hear the reverend, whom I had never met, announce just before his sermon, "I understand that Mr. Wally Frost from California is with us this morning. If he is so disposed, I would like to announce he will be singing for us at our evening service tonight."

Moody Church in Chicago could not afford risks like that. You were first invited to sing for a smaller group and then were approved for the major evening service. There was a thorough check of the sound system for the cavernous auditorium as well as for radio. Several members of my family were in attendance and were seated down front. They were aware that I had been blessed with more volume than quality, so after the service they falteringly inquired as to why I couldn't be heard in the third row. It seems that the sound engineering had gone awry. The song was heard only by the radio audience. That huge building had literally swallowed the sound. The house mike was dead. I had for all intents and purposes panto-mimed my way through three verses of an old-fashioned gospel song. Oh, my!

Not until I got to California did I experience the most revolutionary approach to a church service. Indeed, it took a young preacher with a lot of imagination and vision to dream this one up. As if conducting Sunday morning services under a broiling sun in a drive-in theater were not enough, this fellow came up with the ultra novel idea of having a guest soloist appear in his wheelchair. Not from a normal platform, mind you. But from the roof of the projection booth!

Now I invite you . . . Get yourself a wheelchair. Call four inexperienced ushers, men who are used to handling nothing heavier than the collection plate on Sunday morning. Ask them to elevate you to the roof of the booth by way of an almost vertical stair. "Careful, men. Easy does it." Up and down those stairs was always an incredible journey. Fortunately only three churches in the area invited me to participate in that fashion. I'm not sure Dr. Bob Schuller had visions of a Glass Cathedral in that humble setting. I think we both were thankful for the opportunity to share the simple gospel message in word and song under God's great "Azure Cathedral."

Since I never have thought I had a lot of talent, either musically or otherwise, I have simply wanted to be available to serve God. He has always provided ample opportunities. Over the years it has been physically exhausting. A well-worn cliché seems to fit: I feel like the man who said he would rather wear out than rust out. There is something exhilarating about wearing out for God.

Early on a Sunday morning, twice a month, I head for one of Los Angeles County's juvenile facilities. If you have never been to one, you owe it to yourself to pay a visit. Attend a chapel service some Sunday. I'm sure it could easily be arranged through Christian Jail Workers, one of the agencies serving the spiritual needs of those behind jail walls. If you have a sensitive bone in your body your heart will be broken.

Imagine, if you will, two eight-year-old boys in the front row. Their tousled hair and boyish grins remind you of the boys next door. It's only that the neighbor boys don't dress in identical blue denims, the jail garb. Inquire as to why they are there. Car theft. "Car theft? Neither one of them is big enough to drive a car, let alone steal it."

"No, but together they did. One sat on a box behind the wheel, the other one on the floor working brakes, accelerator—whichever was needed. It worked. Until they got their signals mixed up and crashed into a lamppost."

You can almost assume they are better off in the hall than at home. Maybe the judge will be able to find a good foster home for them. At the moment you are delighted to see them in chapel. You pray earnestly that God will give you something very special to say that will penetrate their crusty little spirits. There have been a lot of kids in the past—a lot tougher than these tenderfeet—who have found a new way of life in this place. Yes, new life in Christ, to be sure.

In the fifth row, second from the aisle, sits a skinny, rawboned kid. He will be 18 next month. There will be no camp assignment or foster home for him. It will be graduation to the "big house." Murder One!

On this particular day a quiet calm prevails over the service. Attendance is voluntary but the place is packed— nearly 200 of them. That usually means there will be a minor disturbance during the hour. Today there is none. At the close of the meeting the response is overwhelming. The kids have really been listening. Some of their lives will change and they will never be sent back to the hall again. Their meeting with God that day is for keeps.

Stan plays the organ softly as the kids file out. He's smiling gratefully. He's British—so much so that the organ music sounds like it has a British accent. He has been faithful to his ministry for many years. The kids love him.

It's been 23 years since I started regular visits twice a month at the juvi halls. Would that I had as many more years to do the same.

On the third Sunday morning it's an entirely different experience. There are two services at this branch of the County Hospital each week. The faithful volunteer chaplains, Charles and Bob, have been serving the needs of the patients all week. On Sunday they usually arrange something special. I don't feel so special, but I'm it.

But the patients in attendance are *really* special. Some are hard-bitten alcoholics who have been recycling through the place for years. The dry-out and subsequent therapy never seem to really "take." One patient is not so hard-bitten; he's only a kid barely out of his teens—his hair is disheveled and his knuckles are white with tension. Two women are sitting in the front row. They are holding hands and crying softly together.

Three or four wheelchair patients are parked around the sides and in front. It's obvious that they have made a real effort to get there. The most notable "parishioners" are the two who have arrived in their beds. One in particular catches my eye. His name is Lonnie. He has only been a patient here for two or three years. His brain was irreparably damaged in a motorcycle accident. Not a word has crossed his lips since. I had to squeeze back a tear when I greeted him and he gave me his maximum response—the slightest kink in the corner of his mouth, and blinking eyes. He chose to come to the church service to give thanks. Thanks for being alive. Thanks for his special relationship with God.

Bob sings. I sing. Mila sings and plays her guitar. Chaplain Charles reads a psalm and Chaplain Bob, not the singer, offers prayer. I open the Book and share. Hazel plays the organ softly as I speak. Tears flow freely. Some very needy people come to grips with the issues of life, death and eternity. I thank God for the very breath with which to share His love with these dear folks. This trip has been a monthly pilgrimage for nearly as long as the ones to the juvenile halls.

Speaking at the missions is a unique experience unparalleled by any other platform. It's not easy to maintain your train of thought when some half-drunken, unshaven down-and-outer stands up in the front row and begins to rant, "You can go to hell! You don't know what you're talking about." He is quickly ushered to an anteroom where he promises to sit quietly for the remainder of the service; then he is allowed to return. He doesn't want to miss out on the post-meeting dinner of bean soup, bread and hot coffee. The old "lighthouse," Pacific Garden Mission on South State Street in Chicago, was the first mission I ever visited. Good thing too. They operate a first-rate program. The man in charge announces rather directly that no nonsense will be tolerated, so things go smoothly. Only one minor deviation: A shrunken wisp of a man stands to his feet and soulfully requests that I sing, "Near to the Heart of God." I don't expect him to denounce the message of the evening.

The old Beacon Street Mission in San Pedro was always a special challenge. You could nearly always expect a cast of characters representing broken and wasted lives. Many a man who was virtually dead walked the aisle of that old "lighthouse" to live again.

The new Long Beach Rescue Mission has a special uniqueness. It is operated by Wayne and Jan, a youthful couple with vision. They bring a touch of class to mission work—cleanliness, good food, family concern, superb organization and outstanding programming. The community accords the mission a place of high regard. It has been a distinct privilege to participate in the program on occasions.

Union Rescue Mission, downtown Los Angeles, has speakers standing in line. You are booked well in advance. A noon visit usually means being on the radio as well. But a little husband-wife place down on Fifth Street seldom had speakers. The two of them, Tom and Annette, paid the rent, cooked the soup, led the singing and alternated with the speaking.

A movie scriptwriter could not have written a crazier scenario. Since Phyl and I were invited to "conduct" the meeting, we were in charge from start to finish. I was to lead the singing, sing a couple of solos and preach. The mission was small; there were probably not more than 15 or 20 in attendance.

Leading the singing there should be no problem. How wrong I was. The loudest, purest voice of the bunch was seated squarely in the middle of the front row. Normally that would be a big help, but this fellow had his own idea of a song service. He was agreeable to singing at the same time—but not the same song. He didn't seem to think it made much difference as long as we were all singing. Tom patiently pointed out the correct page number and quietly urged him to join the rest of us. All to no avail. It was no doubt the most discordant song service I had ever led.

About halfway through the song service an aged gentleman staggered through the door pushing a "borrowed" grocery cart containing all of his worldly possessions. It was immediately apparent that the old man was seriously ill. It was a warm summer night and a ragged, short-sleeved shirt exposed an elbow area that most certainly looked gangrenous. It was an ugly yellowish-green, oozing serum. He slumped wearily on the front bench, gasping heavily. The singing was cut short as he pitched headlong to the floor. Phyl and Annette bolted from the platform to minister to his physical needs. It was difficult to tell if he was breathing. His pulse was virtually imperceptible. His eyes were open and glazed. Normally, emergency help would have been summoned, but that night a quiet tranquility settled over the place. A simple prayer was offered on his behalf and the singing continued.

Annette played the introductory notes to a special number and I began to sing. "I was drifting away on life's pitiless sea, and the angry waves threatened my ruin to be, when away at my side . . ." The mood was broken sharply as the old-timer suddenly leaped to his feet. "You saved my life! You saved my life!" With that he grabbed his cart of belongings and disappeared out the door into the night.

Certainly this was the end of the interruptions! Not quite. I was just getting well into my text. "Whither shall I go from thy spirit? or whither shall I flee from thy presence? If I ascend up into heaven, thou art there: if I make my bed in hell, behold, thou art there" (Ps. 139:7,8).

Suddenly the street door burst open! A wild-eyed man in his early twenties stood silhouetted against the night. His hair was matted, his clothing hung in disarray and fresh blood streaked his unshaven chin. "Where is the back door? I need to get out of here before they catch me!" he cried. A huge buckle attached to a military belt hung menacingly from his clenched fist. He swore crudely.

I turned to Phyl. "Quick, call the police!"

Tom interjected calmly, "Sorry, we don't have a phone."

"Then run out in the street and flag down a black and white." Phyl blanched and stuck to her seat. She wasn't about to go out there with the man's pursuers on the loose. Probably a good thing too. Momentarily they came crashing through the door in hot pursuit. Meanwhile, Tom had gently shown the young man to the back room and was unbolting the alley door.

It was a threatening sight to behold—two muscular street types with eyes flashing fire, stripped to the waist.

Each had an open switchblade in hand. Silently I prayed, "Oh, Lord have mercy on us all." They apparently had some respect for what was going on in the place. Slowly they lowered their weapons and began to back toward the door. The larger would-be assailant mumbled some unintelligible word of apology and they too disappeared into the night.

What in the world are we doing here? I thought. Surely it would have been wiser to have stayed home with the kids.

Later as Phyl and I were leaving the mission, Tom was on his knees at the altar with his arm extended around the shoulder of a young man who knelt with him. We knew why we had come.

The hardest aspect of availability is the hours. Folks just don't seem to have any respect for sleep. I may have been raised on the farm but I could never get used to the idea of getting up with the chickens.

Teaching a Sunday School class at 9:00 A.M. was a breeze compared to some of the other assignments. It was those seven o'clock high school club meetings or equally early businessmen's breakfasts that tested the will. It was definitely agonizing when distance and time required the wheels to be on the road before six. Now that I think about it, there are lots of times the chickens weren't up yet.

Does that kind of thing have its rewards or is it merely an exercise in self-abuse? I recall speaking one morning to a group of more than 200 local high school students. One of their classmates had been killed on the way to school a day or two earlier. That morning a number of fine young people made sure that things were right between their soul and the Saviour.

That makes it worth getting up at any hour.

Father/son and father/daughter affairs have always been favorites of mine. I don't know when I have felt more fulfilled than at a recent banquet at Southern California College. I had been invited to be the guest of my daughters, Becky and Debbie. Seated between them, two of the most beautiful girls in the world, I fairly glowed with pride—the kind God approves of. It was altogether incidental that someone else had invited me—to be the speaker, that is.

I'm equally grateful when my sons are available to share the platform at a breakfast or a dinner. I don't mind being upstaged by those fellows.

I have always been grateful for continuous employment through the years. Although the government has made a big pitch to "hire the handicapped," in practice it has been more fancy than fact. I have had considerable satisfaction in being able to say that I honestly do not recall ever having had to ask for a job. Particularly 25 years ago when jobs for the disabled were relatively hard to come by.

There is no doubt in my mind that God is the provider and prepares the way for us. I think He enjoys working through our availability.

Once I was working on a job between jobs. I didn't really have a plan as to my next move. It was hard, dirty work. When a rush job came into the shop I was required to work 16 to 18 hours a day. On this particular day my job was wiring an electrical sign. I was filthy. That's the only way I could be described—filthy.

As I rolled through the door at home around six, the phone rang. My sister-in-law, Elvina, was on the line. "How would you like to speak at the Girls Athletic Association banquet for Valley Christian High this year?"

"Oh, I guess I could do that. How many people will be there?" I felt more comfortable with small groups.

"Not many," she said. "Probably the 15 or 20 girls getting their awards and their families."

Why, sure. I was interested. "When is it?"

"They are already eating. The speaker called a few minutes ago and bowed out with an emergency. I was asked to call you. I'm sure glad you can do it."

Had I said yes without getting all of the details? I almost felt like I'd been trapped. "I can't come that soon. I'm really scroungy. It will take me quite a while to get cleaned up and get there," I protested. Maybe I was off the hook.

"We'll wait and—THANK YOU." The phone was dead.

Somehow they stretched out the program so that the MC was ready the moment I rolled through the door. "And now, it gives me great pleasure to introduce our speaker of the evening. . . ." The few girls and their families turned out to be something between two and three hundred. My speech turned out to be two or three minutes. No, not really, more like 30. Some of the folks were only wishing it would be two or three.

A day or two later the principal of Valley Christian High called me. "We have a teaching position available in Social Science next year. Would you be interested?"

I tried to sound mildly interested. Sure, I would think about it and call back. I let a couple of days pass to give the appearance of respectability. But I couldn't wait to dial that phone number. It was the beginning of a long career as teacher and counselor. A door had been opened that no man could close. Several of my friends in wheelchairs had applied for teaching positions for years without success.

After a beautiful nine-year tenure at V.C.H. I began to think it might be permanent.

Watchmaking was still an avocation to augment my income. One day a total stranger left a clock to be repaired. He had stopped by several times to pick it up but it was never finished. Finally he caught me at home during the dinner hour. He volunteered to leave and return yet another day.

"No, sit down and let me take a look at the thing." One operation with pliers and tweezers and it was ticking like new. Took all of a minute.

"How much do I owe you?"

"Nothing. You saw how simple it was to fix."

He pressed. "Hey, they wanted $19.50 at the department store. Let me give you something."

Since he was so anxious to leave some money I accommodated him. "O.K. Give me a buck." I had a reputation for "overcharging" which resulted in a lot of work but not too much income. He seemed to be more than pleased and stayed on to pass the time of day.

He knew about a counseling job opening at a local community college. Would I mind if he told them about me? No, of course not. What could it hurt? He left. The very next day the phone rang.

I am now nearing the end of my sixteenth year at Cerritos Community College, Norwalk, California. The phone number is 860-2 . . . On second thought, the phone rings too much already. Drop me a line. I'll call you.

Another door had been opened. It was a simple matter of stepping through. When and if another door opens, I'm ready.

Doors can be closed as well as opened. In 1966 the concept of establishing a Christian High School in Zambia in Central Africa was formulated. It was encouraging to discover that authorities from the States were of the opinion that "no one felt that your disability was of such a nature that it would hinder you from doing an effective job . . ." The challenge called for building the school, staffing and administrating the operation. The executive secretary of the mission and I had an understanding, but God knew better. That door was closed.

The trip through life has been one big, glorious adventure. It's awfully hard to relate it in the first person without sounding a little like an egomaniac.

"But God forbid that I should glory . . ." (Gal. 6:14).

Chapter 10
Give Me That Old-Time Religion

The old Negro spiritual had it about right: "Give me
that old-time religion, give me that old-time religion . . . it's
good enough for me." I don't know much about the more
subtle points of the theology of the songwriter but if it was
good for his brother, his mother and his father he made a
good decision in deciding it was good enough for him.

As parents, Phyl and I are the first to recognize that
God does not have any grandchildren. However, parents
and family should be the most likely to play the role of
"midwife." I have no idea how many parents have asked,
"How did you do it? What was your secret?" It is no secret.
To us the answer has been obvious—what was good for
our parents was good enough for us. Those parents who
decide that the faith of their fathers is not for them find the
path of parenthood laden with disaster. Not only do they
deny God at every turn in the road themselves but their
children are living witnesses to Dad and Mom's testimony.

I am sure our parents offered volumes of prayer on our
behalf. They saturated themselves with instruction from
the Book. When God spoke to them from His Word,
"Therefore shall ye lay up these my words in your heart
and in your soul . . . And ye shall teach them your children, speaking of them when thou sittest in thine house,

and when thou walkest by the way, when thou liest down, and when thou risest up" (Deut. 11:18,19), they believed it. They practiced it.

One of Phyl's most beautiful recollections of her father is the many times she passed his bedroom door and saw him kneeling there by his bed, speaking in a mixture of broken English and Dutch. He earnestly petitioned the very throne of God on behalf of his 10 children and more than 50 grandchildren. Even today every letter from her 90-year-old mother is signed "God's Procting [protecting] Care." She has had 90 years of evidence that God does protect and care.

My father was inclined to live it as much as talk it. He was often accused of carrying honesty too far. "Ernie, you'll never get anywhere in this world. You are too honest." He had a reputation for turning the other cheek. Many of the neighbors often faulted him for that too. All except Ernie Bowman, a next-door neighbor.

Dad's cow had wandered through a break in the fence and wound up in Bowman's cornfield. Bowman was angry. He spoke abusively to Dad about the incident. Dad practiced a little "soft answer" theology. In his frustration the angry cow owner decked Dad with a sucker punch. Dad practiced a little "other cheek" theology. His manly response was simply, "Ernie, I'll come back for my cow another day. You may be feeling better then." The incident was over. At least seemingly so.

Thirty years later Dad was driving along a street in southern California, more than 2,000 miles from the cornfield episode. He noticed a familiar name on a mailbox—Ernie Bowman. No, it couldn't be. Or could it? He checked. A small world suddenly got much smaller. The same Ernie B. answered the door. He was in a completely different frame of mind. Addressing Dad he said, "Ernie, do you remember that time I punched you in the jaw? I want you to know that I'm now a Christian too. Your response to my ugly temper that day did more to get me to consider becoming a Christian than any other one experience in my life. I just want to thank you, Ernie, for showing me some real Christianity in action."

Dad didn't preach much but he practiced a lot.

My precious mother was a disciple of Solomon. She was thoroughly convinced that all the answers to the problems of youth could be found in his popular collection of proverbs: "Fools despise wisdom and instruction" (Prov. 1:7); "For whom the Lord loveth he correcteth" (3:12); "A soft answer turneth away wrath" (15:1); "He that spareth his rod hateth his son" (13:24); "When a man's ways please the Lord, he maketh even his enemies to be at peace with him" (16:7); "A merry heart doeth good like a medicine" (17:22); and so many more. You'll just have to sit down and read the book. It may surprise you what you've been missing. But the one I'm still having a tough time getting a handle on is: "Even a fool, when he holdeth his peace, is counted wise: and he that shutteth his lips is esteemed a man of understanding" (17:28).

Of all the proverbs that our moms and dads lived and died by, none summed up their approach to parenting better than 22:6: "Train up a child in the way he should go: and when he is old, he will not depart from it." They believed it. We believe it. God's Word says it. That settles it.

It really makes no difference how close a walk with God the parents may have. It still boils down to an individual choice. Do you or don't you? Will you or won't you? I must have been about 11 when I willed.

My older sister Maryann had returned from Bible college for the vacation break. The farm was a busy place in the summertime. Plenty of work for everyone. But this was a slow, lazy day; when the hot wind of July stands still, everything else is inclined to, also. My big sister was cleaning the stuffy attic and I watched. Attics are curious places.

We talked. It was an unforgettable conversation. That morning for the first time I realized that being born into the Frost family did not mean that I had also been born into the family of God. There, in simple childlike faith, I received the greatest gift that is available to a person. I whispered a simple prayer and accepted Jesus into my heart and life. I don't recall the exact date but the event has been recorded for eternity.

The first real test to that faith came during those frustrating years in the veterans hospital. Thanks be to God some pretty significant people intersected my life at that time, including my sweet Phyl, who is and always will be *number one*.

There was Joe Ganns, of course, my quadraplegic friend. Joe proved to me more thoroughly than anyone I have ever met that the statement, "the joy of the Lord is your strength" (Neh. 8:10), is a valid contention. Circumstances notwithstanding, God makes no mistakes.

And then there was "Pat." He had been nailed in the spine by a machine gun bullet. It wouldn't have been so bad if it had been the enemy, but it happened during basic training while he was navigating a barbed-wire course on his belly. Some eager "buck-sergeant" was going to make those raw recruits crawl low or else.

You would have expected "Pat" to be bitter beyond words. Instead I think it was he who called my attention to a special message from the psalmist: "He delighteth not in the strength of the horse: he taketh not pleasure in the legs of a man. The Lord taketh pleasure in them that [reverence] him, in those that hope in his mercy. Praise the Lord" (Ps. 147:10-12). We have always appreciated those words. Were they written especially for us? Chaplain "Pat" Patterson has faithfully served for many years as a hospital chaplain from his "chrome chariot."

Serving the spiritual needs of the three of us there at the hospital was volunteer Chaplain Ernie Miller. A more kindly, Christ-like saint we will never meet. He had served in the trenches in the first Big War. German mustard gas had seared his lungs so much that one had been removed and the other was badly scarred. Ernie literally "whistled" from bed to bed. His conversation was punctuated with frequent gasps. He may have sounded like a gasketless air pump when he talked but there was never anything on his lips but Good News. I vaguely recall that it was Chaplain Ernie who called my attention to a simple prayer from the lips of David the psalmist: "It is good for me that I have been afflicted; that I might learn thy statutes" (Ps. 119:71).

I never thought I would ever be able to fully understand the magnitude of that prayer. As the years have passed there have been not only paralysis but uncountable attacks of gallstones, kidney stones and gout. These too have served to remind me that I am still learning and will continue to learn what God means when He says, "when thou passest through the waters, I will be with thee; and through the rivers, they shall not overflow thee" (Isa. 43:2).

There are many well-meaning people who have insisted to me that "if you just had enough faith" I'd be healed. Well, I don't have a doubt in the world that there are many people who experience spontaneous remission from a great variety of ailments. The same God who made this world and put the sun and the moon in their orbits can certainly undertake to restore the most feeble among us. God has not gone back on any part of His Word. If the prayer of faith saved the sick in A.D. 60 it can obviously deliver them today. I *know* God can heal; I'm just not sure why or when or who.

I had an experience that proved to me beyond shadow of doubt that He can heal. Returning from a speaking assignment one Sunday morning before the family had returned from church I found eggs boiling on the stove. Evidently someone had forgotten to turn off the gas. I thought I would help: shell the eggs and put them in the refrigerator. My mind must have been in limbo. While transferring the kettle from the stove to the sink I placed it on the countertop in such a manner as to pour the three to four quarts of near-boiling water right down my front—stomach, abdomen and parts below.

Someone listening might have thought I was swearing. At the top of my voice I uttered the most spontaneous prayer of my life. "PRAISE THE LORD! THANK YOU, JESUS!" And with that I ripped off every stitch of clothes. Calling the church where I thought Phyl should be I gave an emergency message for her to rush home.

An hour later she ambled in unsuspectingly. She never had gone to church. Providentially she had visited a needy friend who needed Phyl's ministration more than the wife needed another sermon. Phyl is not given to alarmist reactions but seeing the bright red skin already beginning to marble with a blister-like ripple she declared firmly, "Let's get to the emergency room as quickly as we can! You are in trouble!" She proceeded to predict that I would not be able to work for weeks. Infection was a certainty if I tried to wear a belt before it was healed. Normally I would have expected her to say, "Oh, that's not so bad. You'll be OK in a day or two."

I dared not put on my trousers all the way so we let things drape around me so I was fairly decent for the emergency waiting room. It must have been close to an hour before I was invited into the examining area. The doctor inquired tersely. "And what's your problem?"

Hadn't he read the chart? I had explained the whole episode in great detail to the E.R. nurse. I gently pulled aside my loosely draped clothes. "I've been burned," I said.

His next response was even more laconic, "Where?"

"Right here, all down my front and over my . . ."

He looked quizzically, attempting to locate the area. "I see no evidence of a burn. Are you sure?"

This was getting to be embarrassing. I had resisted looking at the area. Finally looking down I began to understand the doctor's seemingly peculiar behavior. At first I patted gently, then I slapped. Finally I scratched! It felt perfect. It looked perfect. It was perfect!

He rubbed his head and gave me the strangest look as he invited me to leave. "But, Doctor," I stammered, "I *was* burned. I really was. All I can say is, you and I have just witnessed a modern-day miracle."

He was still scratching his head as he left the examination room. I suspect he was thinking he had futilely examined another one of those "crazies."

I recalled my prayer. "Praise the Lord. Thank you, Jesus." What had James the Just written about "effectual fervent prayer?" It was as though God was saying, "Yes, I heal, but only I know why or when or who."

I have often wondered about my many brushes with death; then, having been spared, how does this physical infirmity fit the picture? People often ask, "Why do you think God did that to you?" Let it be unmistakably clear: *God did not do this to me.* God is the author of only that which is good and perfect. "Far be it from God, that he should do wickedness; and from the Almighty, that he should commit iniquity" (Job 34:10).

Do I understand it? Of course not. The glass through which I view life is no less opaque than that through which the apostle Paul was looking. I do not pretend to understand the full implications of this "thorn in the flesh." But this I do know, His grace *has been* sufficient for me (see 2 Cor. 12:9). It can be for you too.

If the enemy of my body, my soul and my spirit plotted this evil thing against me, and I believe he did, God meant it for good. Remember Job? Having suffered calamity beyond description did he not answer, "Though he slay me, yet will I trust in him" (Job 13:15)? And in the final analysis, "So the Lord blessed the latter end of Job more than his beginning. . . . Also the Lord gave Job twice as much as he had before" (Job 42:12,10).

My friends, the best is yet to come!

Someone has said that for parents to establish a Christian family is the greatest contribution that can be made to society. No question about it. I don't think it requires statistics to prove the point. How many people who overcrowd our penal institutions were reared in homes where God was honored, His Word read and Christ lifted up? Witness the true family histories of the Jutes and the Edwards.

A fellow by the name of Jutes lived in upper New York state. He was a non-believer. No Christian talk at his house. He married a girl of similar persuasion. A careful study of their genealogy records more than a thousand descendants. What a record! More than 300 of them died early in life. Nearly 200 turned to prostitution. More than a hundred spent a total of 1,300 years in penal institutions. There were more than a hundred drunkards. The cost to the state was well in excess of a million dollars. There is no evidence that any member of the family made a significant contribution to the world.

A thoughtful young chap lived in the same neighborhood, Jonathan Edwards by name. He believed. Christian teaching would be the talk around his house. He married a girl of similar persuasion. A study of their family tree reveals some startling contrasts. Of the more than 700 descendants some 300 became faithful ministers of the gospel. Nearly 80 became college professors with more than a dozen ascending to a college presidency. There were some 60 authors, three U.S. congressmen, one vice president of the United States. Apart from Aaron Burr, a grandson of the Edwards' union, the total family tree made outstanding contributions to society.

Why will parents give their children anything but God?

The heartbeat of home resides in Mother. "Who can find a virtuous woman? for her price is far above rubies" (Prov. 31:10). My children have been blessed beyond measure. Their instruction "in the nurture and admonition of the Lord" (Eph. 6:4) really began at her knee. They learned early that "Jesus" was not a curse word. It was indeed the name of the loving Son of God who loves children and invites all of them to come to Him "for of such is the kingdom of heaven" (Matt. 19:14).

What did Jesus mean when He invited the children to come to Him? I take it He meant the same thing He means when He invites all men to "come unto me, all ye that labour and are heavy laden, and I will give you rest" (Matt. 11:28). Jesus invites the littlest child to receive Him. If a child has learned the difference between yes and no, between right and wrong, he is capable of opening his heart and inviting the Saviour to come in (see Rev. 3:20). As parents we thank God that each of our children "confessed" and "believed" before they left the instruction of the home for more formal education.

It was at their mother's knee that they first learned,

"Thy word have I hid in mine heart, that I might not sin against thee" (Ps. 119:11). Yes, indeed, "her children arise up, and call her blessed; her husband also, and he praiseth her" (Prov. 31:28). Oh my! How we love that woman. *Oh, yes, God, how I love her.*

Men, do yourselves a favor. Love your children. More than that, love your wives. When is the last time you hid flowers in the refrigerator and listened for that delightful squeal when she discovered them? When is the last time you drove her to the top of a hill and watched the lights of the city? When did you ever . . . ? Try it. It pays off like a blue chip coupon. Paul who didn't exactly push for marriage, provided some profound advice, "So ought men to love their wives as their own bodies. He that loveth his wife loveth himself" (Eph. 5:28). I tell you, men. Paul was right on.

Our house was never known as a place lacking in communication. One preteen who had shared the dinner hour with us was heard to say, "How does anybody hear what anybody else says? Everyone is talking at the same time." It was not an easy question to answer. Dinner was din and more din; I guess you could say it was "din-din." But we all understood and loved it.

Around the table is the best place in the world to learn that "man shall not live by bread alone, but by every word . . . of God" (Matt. 4:4). There you have a perfect opportunity to explain what the psalmist was getting at when he asked where and how a young guy or gal could get his act together. How? By listening and paying attention to the instruction that God gives in His Word. Read it for yourself—Psalm 119:9.

Recently I heard a rather unbelievable statistic. Fathers spend, on the average, less than 10 minutes a week talking to the individual child! Think about it. That figures out to something like a minute and 25 seconds a day. What can a dad say to his son in less than a minute and a half? Oh, I know, "Get lost." "I'm too busy." "Go play jacks on the freeway." One of the greatest gifts a parent can offer his child is the gift of time. Time to play. Time to love. Time to work. Time to listen. Time to instruct. Time to be.

One of the greatest legacies passed on to our family by our parents was their unselfish devotion of time to their children. When Dad put aside his profitable engineering career to become a dirt farmer I can hear him saying, "I have no greater joy than to hear that my children walk in truth" (3 John 4). As parents we early committed ourselves to sacrifice of time.

The establishment of priorities has always been a struggle for us and probably always will be. Consequently one of the most oft-repeated words from the Book at our house came from the very lips of Jesus Himself. He was giving one of His better known public addresses, His Sermon on the Mount. "But seek ye first the kingdom of God, and his righteousness; and all these things shall be added unto you" (Matt. 6:33). Talk about social reform! Can you imagine the radical change in our society if every person alive were to take Jesus at His word on that one issue alone?

It has been more than obvious to this family that once Dad got his goofed-up priorities halfway straightened around, that admonition became a living reality. When football fortunes were first, my whole world went sour. When God finally was able to get my attention, He added and added and added to my experience; even multiplied in the area of athletics. And not just actual experience but vicariously through the athletic and spiritual adventures of our children.

It is amazing how youngsters prosper through the nourishment of praise. I would to God that I could take back every critical word; that I would have listened louder to Paul's admonition to a father, "Provoke not your children to wrath" (Eph. 6:4). But just listening part-time has yielded dividends beyond description.

To praise the children is one thing. Teaching them to praise God is quite another. A good place to begin is with conversational prayer. Around the table we often talked to God as though He were another person seated with the family. Only a sentence at a time. Spontaneously. No now-I-lay-me-down-to-sleep sort of thing. Just us and God. Talking. Visiting. Being friends. There is real comfort for children to feel that God lives at their house. Right there with them. A reality in their lives. The concept is best epitomized by a child's conceptualization of nightly prayer, reporting on her first moments after bedtime, "I just move over and make room for God in bed with me. We talk until I go to sleep."

You as parents can sleep well when you know your kids have a firm grasp on some rules. I think I can honestly say that Phyl and I have not spent a sleepless night ever worrying about any of our offspring. We didn't have a whole lot of rules at our house. It seems like the rules were flexible and usually tailored to fit the occasion. Some of our rules were good and some not so good. A few of the rules were not ours. With these we couldn't miss. One has been around for a while. It works: "Honour thy father and thy mother: that thy days may be long upon the land which the Lord thy God giveth thee" (Exod. 20:12). The apostle Paul considered the idea worthy of repetition and elaboration: "Children, obey your parents in the Lord: for this is right. Honour thy father and mother; which is the first commandment with promise; that it may be well with thee, and thou mayest live long on the earth" (Eph. 6:1-3).

We praise God that He has kept His covenant with us through the years and is continuing and will continue until the end of our times. His promise bears repeating, "Train up a child in the way he should go: and when he is old, he will not depart from it" (Prov. 22:6). No cause for despair. No reason to worry. God is in control. And hear this reinforcement of our faith, "Being confident of this very thing, that he which hath begun a good work in you will perform it until the day of Jesus Christ" (Phil. 1:6). Yes we can be confident. Yes God does perform. How praiseworthy are His precious promises!

Building self-confidence in children is a difficult task under even the very best of circumstances. The stresses of this generation cause the hearts of many to fail them for fear. Any child, any person, who incorporates the Word of

God into his experience gets a head start on those who don't. "For God hath not given us the spirit of fear; but of power, and of love, and of a sound mind" (2 Tim. 1:7). "Ye are of God, little children, and have overcome them: because greater is he that is in you, than he that is in the world" (1 John 4:4). Can our children face the world with confidence? No doubt about it, "For whatsoever is born of God overcometh the world: and this is the victory that overcometh the world, even our faith" (1 John 5:4). "If God be for us, who can be against us?" (Rom. 8:31).

Thank you, God, for that gift of faith. It sure anchors the process of raising a family.

I would not want the reader to get the idea that we have somehow "arrived." Be assured we are still on the way. The jury is still out. The whole story will be known only in eternity. If one of you were to meet any one of our children on the street tomorrow, the circumstances of that moment might incline you to ask, "Is this a product of that home I was reading about?" Be patient. God is still working. We are still praying. The end will be far better than the beginning.

Please don't try to measure the magnitude of our God by the microcosm of our experience. God does not allow us the luxury of using our failures and inconsistencies as a place to hide from the scrutiny of His Word. God knows how desperately I would like to have retracted the many words and actions that have been offensive to anyone, even in the slightest sense. To those to whom I have never had the opportunity or thought to say, "I'm sorry, please forgive me," I say it now. To those who may have impinged upon my sensitivities I publicly say, "I forgive you." Unfortunately we mortals seem to possess only the capacity to forgive. Thank God, He forgives *and* forgets.

I keep remembering the expression of the greatest saint of all, Saint Paul. Describing the struggle between his old nature and his new, he confessed, "For the good that I would I do not: but the evil which I would not, that I do" (Rom. 7:19). What a beautiful world if we could see each other in the light of Paul's dilemma and forgive accordingly. How much more beautiful for each of us to be irreversibly convinced, even as Paul was "persuaded, that neither death, nor life, nor angels, nor principalities, nor powers, nor things present, nor things to come, nor height, nor depth, nor any other creature, shall be able to separate us from the love of God, which is in Christ Jesus our Lord" (Rom 8:38,39). I am so persuaded.

As a young boy working the soil from season to season the immutable laws of this universe were indelibly fixed upon my impressionable mind. It was not difficult to observe that a kernel of corn or grain always yielded in kind. Not just kernel for kernel or grain for grain, but the result was always a profusion of corn or barley from a single seed. It was never different. To a barefoot boy it was pretty apparent that thistle seeds bring forth more thistles. Ouch, but how they did hurt!

Amazingly enough there are untold millions who have never learned the law of planting and harvest. They have the mistaken notion that they can plant thistle seeds and reap wheat. If my kids decide to sow some thistle seed it's a cinch they know what the result will be. They cannot, I cannot fool God. As the old saying goes, "It's not nice to fool Mother Nature." Well, nature is not Mother, but God is God. His laws are irrevocable: "They that plow iniquity, and sow wickedness, reap the same" (Job 4:8).

I find it incomprehensible that so many think they can thumb their noses at God and get away with it. Allowing for those who do not believe in God to be so foolish ("The fool hath said in his heart, There is no God [Ps. 14:1]), the vast host of God-believers ought to recognize that you can't fool with the rules. They are only kidding themselves when they try. How much more directly could God tell us? "Be not deceived; God is not mocked: for whatsoever a man soweth, that shall he also reap. For he that soweth to his flesh shall of the flesh reap corruption; but he that soweth to the Spirit shall of the Spirit reap life everlasting" (Gal. 6:7,8). Or as *The Living Bible* translates it, "Don't be misled; remember that you can't ignore God and get away with it: a man will always reap just the kind of crop he sows!

If he sows to please his own wrong desires, he will be planting seeds of evil and he will surely reap a harvest of spiritual decay and death; but if he plants the good things of the Spirit, he will reap the everlasting life which the Holy Spirit gives him."

How well we all know that you can lead the proverbial horse to water without getting him to drink. Once the family game plan has been established and everyone knows the rules you as a parent have pretty well done your job. Your kids now know your set of values almost better than you. Yours had better be worthy of emulation. It's axiomatic: If they don't follow your example, your set of values, they'll follow someone else's. "Therefore, . . . stand fast, and hold the traditions which you have been taught" (2 Thess. 2:15).

And if they don't? Go to your garden and eat worms? No, don't do that. Continue to claim God's promises for your children. "The just man walketh in his integrity: his children are blessed after him" (Prov. 20:7). As parents we must remember that one of the great attributes with which we have been endowed by our Creator is a will that gives all of us the freedom of choice. It is entirely possible that any one of our children may choose to "journey into a far country, and there [waste] his substance with riotous living" (Luke 15:13). That happens to be one of the "luxuries" that goes with freedom of choice. Thanks be to God He made us each a free moral agent. With that freedom we make our choices. As parents we have made our choices. With our choices we have experienced our share of failures as well as successes. With God's help we have faithfully attempted to lift up a standard for the family. It is our earnest prayer that our children will carry that standard forward and pass it on to the next generation, if the Lord should tarry.

Joshua said it better than we: "Now therefore fear the Lord, and serve him in sincerity and in truth . . . And if it seem [wrong] unto you to serve the Lord, choose you this day whom ye will serve; . . . but as for me and my house, we will serve the Lord" (Josh. 24:14,15).

Chapter 11
Strike Four!

"Eet's coming! Soon. Zee revolooshun eez shur to come. And when it does, I am going to shoot zum people. Zee first weel be Beely Gram. The next will be zee prezee-dent of zees Yoonited States," (no longer in office, by the way). "And zee next wan weel be YOU!"

The man was wild-eyed with rage. The blood vessels on his temples stood out like twisted garden worms. White saliva etched his lips. He was obviously very angry. How had I ignited his fuse? I had simply mentioned the magic word, "Jesus."

I don't suppose he would have been the least bit upset if I had cursed him, using the name. It had all begun so quietly. He had entered my office with a broad smile on his face. "Meester Frost, how would you like to geeve a donashun for zee speshul speaker?" He went on to explain that he was raising money to bring a well-known communist speaker to the area. When I indicated that I was something less than enthusiastic he gloatingly replied that one of my colleagues had given him the sizeable sum of $25.

I would not be outdone. "I'll tell you what I'm going to do. I'll give you $26. Yes, sir, 26 bucks." His eyes fairly flashed with glee. He really hadn't expected me to give more than 25¢. This was far beyond his wildest imagination.

"Yes, I'll give you the money—if you will go out and get a speaker who will counter your Marxist friend with the teachings of one Jesus of Nazareth." You would have thought I had insulted his mother, his father and his brother all in one breath.

He leaped from his chair. Taking the stance of a rifle-toting Green Beret he began to rant about the coming "revolooshun."

So many have declared themselves to be the enemy of God. Even more have made no declaration at all. They simply shrug their shoulders and exist. They seem totally oblivious to Jesus' words that "he that is not with me is against me" (Matt. 12:30).

"Come now, and let us reason together, saith the Lord" (Isa. 1:18). Living in a day in history when man's best efforts are yielding the greatest deficits of all time should give pause for another look. Economics? Really of very little concern. Consider the psychological, moral and spiritual bankruptcy on every hand. You and I without God can do so little to reverse the trends. If true, why not be reasonable and do what we can about our individual state.

But you say, "I'm not such a bad guy. Surely I'm as good as my neighbor or maybe even a little better. God ought to be more than happy about that." Unfortunately, all that goodness is not quite enough. God has told us very simply in His Word that we have all violated His standard of goodness. We have all "come short of the glory of God" (Rom. 3:23).

There are others who may say, "Hey, I am the world's number one disaster. I'm sure that I am beyond redemption." The apostle Paul must have had similar feelings, crying out, "Oh wretched man that I am! who shall deliver me?" (Rom. 7:24). Just as the "all" who have fallen short is all-encompassing, so is Paul's pronouncement that "there is therefore now *no* condemnation to them which are in Christ Jesus" (Rom. 8:1), all-inclusive. That means you too.

Some of my problems with school authorities during my teenage years stemmed from my close friendship with a local "Peck's bad boy." It was simple guilt by association. Sparing the details, my young friend was desperately in need of a rehabilitative process, and cared less about it than anybody I had ever known. One night, after more than two years of persistent invitation, he agreed to attend a Christian Boys Club with me. He figured it wasn't a church so what could it hurt to go.

That night "Huck" became a new creature in Christ. A new person. A new personality. New behavioral patterns. New motives. New desires. After that his story was legend. The town gossips had a field day. The skeptics predicted it would only last for weeks, at best a few months. "Huck" died in two years. In that short period of his new life he left an impact on the community that has had reverberations to the ends of the earth. It's been nearly 40 years but people are still talking about the amazing transformation. Did it pay for "Huck" to trust Christ? Yes it did. For more than two tremendous years. For generations to come. For eternity.

Remember Red? The drunk who used to come to the coffee shop to sleep off his binge? He really wanted out of the pit which he had dug for himself. He had tried it all, both everything to get into the pit as well as everything to get out. Nothing worked. He tried all of the reforming arts. Even church. Nothing worked until he gave up on himself, surrendered his self-will and tried Christ. The transformation was mind-boggling. Again the skeptics predicted momentary relapse. It's been something like 40 years and most of Red's detractors have passed on, but Red is still carrying on. No relapse, no backsliding, no turning back.

He probably epitomizes the regenerative process better than any man I have ever known. "He brought me up also out of an horrible pit, out of the miry clay, and set my feet upon a rock, and established my goings" (Ps. 40:2). "I am come that they might have life, and that they might have it more abundantly" (John 10:10). "My peace I give unto you: not as the world giveth" (John 14:27). "Thou wilt keep him in perfect peace, whose mind is stayed on thee: because he trusteth in thee" (Isa. 26:3). Red has experienced all of this, and much more, because he has been faithful to his decision to follow Jesus. So have thousands more. For them it has been from the pit to the pinnacle.

Whether you have been living in abject misery or whether you feel your personal goodness gives you a feeling of relative contentment remember, "There is a way that seemeth right unto a man, but the end thereof are the ways of death" (Prov. 16:25). There is no other way apart from God's way. You will never find that "perfect peace," that life "more abundantly," that solid footing of rock-like stability, that life-changing newness, apart from Jesus' simple injunction, "Except a man be born again, he cannot see the kingdom of God" (John 3:3).

The other night I went to a dinner which featured some of the outstanding athletes from across the United States. Two of them had a special part in the program. They are two of the greatest athletes that have ever mounted a dais since the first Olympiad in ancient Greece. Having achieved the pinnacle of success in their respective arenas they then asked, "Is this all there is? Surely there must be more." After trying everything conceivable they decided to try Jesus. Both of these men found what had eluded them all their lives, that "peace I give unto you." Not until they permitted God to meet the deepest need of the life experience did they find that peace.

Who are these men who have committed the rest of their lives to sharing this message with the world? No one who has followed sports with a modicum of interest would fail to recognize the names. They are Jerry Lucas and Rosie Grier of professional basketball and football fame respectively. They now fully understand what Jesus was talking about when He said, "What is a man profited, if he shall gain the whole world, and lose his own soul?" (Matt. 16:26).

I have no doubt that many readers have been trying to "hang in there at the plate" with great determination. Satan is probably the best curve-ball pitcher of all time. He's chuckling to himself at his legendary strike-out record. Perhaps you are feeling like you have only one strike left. Or perhaps worse, you may feel as if you have already just plain struck out.

My friend, a lot of us feel like we struck out in life. That's it. Strike three. We've had it. The ball game is over. Pack up your gear and forget it. No hope. Not so with God! When the cares and affairs of this world seemingly have you down for the count, God lovingly invites you to step back up to the plate. His is the only grace in this world that invites you to get to your feet, step to the plate, and offers you another chance at the bat.

If it has been good for my mother, my father, "Huck," Red, Jerry, Rosie and me, if it has been good for the untold millions who have come by the way of the cross, my friend, it is good enough for you.

Before you put this book down, wouldn't you like to experience the joy, the peace, the satisfaction that goes with being a member of the family of God? It is such a simple, uncomplicated thing to do. It doesn't require money, membership, or special pledges. Jesus quietly invites you to "Come unto me . . . my yoke is easy, and my burden is light" (Matt. 11:28,30).

All He asks is a simple recognition of a few facts.

1. "For God so loved the world [YOU], that he gave his only begotten Son, that whosoever believeth in him should not perish, but have everlasting life" (John 3:16).

2. "For all have sinned, and come short of the glory of God (Rom. 3:23).

3. "For the wages of sin is death; but the *gift of God* is eternal life through Jesus Christ our Lord" (Rom. 6:23, italics added).

4. "If thou shalt confess with thy mouth the Lord

Jesus, and shalt believe in thine heart that God hath raised him from the dead, thou shalt be saved. For with the heart man believeth unto righteousness; and with the mouth confession is made unto salvation" (Rom. 10:9,10).

5. "But as many as received him, to them gave he power to become the sons of God, even to them that *believe* on his name" (John 1:12, italics added).

Having recognized these facts, all God asks is that you come sincerely with a simple prayer on your lips, "God be merciful to me a sinner" (Luke 18:13).

Perhaps you would like to amplify that prayer and make it a little more personal. Just you and God. You might want to say something like this:

"Lord Jesus, I believe what you have said in your Word. I believe you died for me and have paid for my sin upon the cross of Calvary. I am truly sorry for my sin. I do earnestly repent of that sin. I now invite you into my life. I receive you as my Lord and my Saviour. I now belong to you.

"Thank you for your mercy. Thank you for your grace. Thank you for receiving me just as I am into the family of God. I am now determined to live for you and serve you all the days of my life. In Jesus' name. Amen."

If you have prayed that prayer and you would like to receive information that will be helpful in your growth and development in the Lord, you may write to me at:

Wally Frost
P.O. Box 15005
Long Beach, CA 90815

You will receive the material at no expense to you.

Life for my family and me has been one grand adventure in faith. God has been faithful. Praise God you have decided to join in that adventure with us. We now face the world together with this confidence, that it is "not by might, nor by power, *but by my spirit*, saith the Lord" (Zech. 4:6, italics added).

Praise God He has given each of us a "STRIKE FOUR"—and more!